MW01172967

PRAISE FOR TRANSFORM

Debbie Tannenbaum is a courageous educator and committed lifelong learner. She is not afraid to take risks in her quests for professional growth and the advancement of student learning, and TRANSFORM: Techy Notes to Make Learning Sticky is just the latest example of this. In TRANSFORM, Debbie gives us an inside look at her professional journey: the highs, lows, challenges, and victories that come with being a growing educator. She also gets practical, sharing invaluable insights regarding the tools and strategies that give students better access, comprehension, and opportunities for creative expression than ever before. Wherever you are in your professional practice, TRANSFORM will inspire you to take that next step.

Tim Cavey - Host of Teachers on Fire Podcast,
8th Grade Teacher and Middle School Vice Principal

I have to tell you that from the moment I began to read Debbie's book, "TRANSFORM: Techy Notes to Make Learning Sticky", it was like I was part of the journey that is Debbie's story. Certainly, we can all agree there are many books about technology in education. However, I found that with this book Debbie invited us to share in her challenges, her epiphanies, her victories, and her moments of coaching others to experience their own triumphs just as well. One of the things I enjoyed most was the authenticity with which Debbie tells her story. In a world where sometimes, what's shared through writing resembles a PR statement, Debbie brings her own style of authenticity and relevance that connects with each of us as we live our lives. Simply, this book is real and tells not only of how we can all "push restart" and begin again with technology, but also how Debbie began again in her personal life. As someone that has been blessed to serve in education in various roles and at different levels, I can share with you from my years of experience that real innovation doesn't come from information and ideas alone. It's our understanding of how we can all honor not just the technology, but more importantly the stories of educators that make the technology come alive for students every day. I challenge you to get this book, go deep with it, learn from it and be inspired by Debbie's story. In doing so I believe that you as well will be inspired to transform in your own journey as an educator and impact maker.

Vernon Wright - Entrepreneur/Speaker/NLP, Life Coach/Consultant/Leader/
Educational Influencer, Founder of ZeroApologyZone.com,
TheWrightLeader.com (@TheWrightLeader)

TRANSFORM: Techy Notes to Make Learning Sticky had me hooked from the very first chapter! This book is a collection of personal stories, technology resources, and thought-provoking ideas to truly transform the educational quality we are delivering to our students in all schools today. Regardless of your experience with technology, while reading this book, every educator will learn how to implement a variety of technological tools to increase the autonomy and voice of all students in the classroom and to inspire you to use technology as a personal growth tool for you. The way Debbie incorporates her own authentic voice and experiences into the book will captivate you as the reader as she creates an experience that builds your confidence to incorporate technology no matter what your role is in education!

Lindsay Titus - K-12 Behavior Specialist,
Mindset Coach & Speaker with DEFINE YOUniversity

I am a firm believer that people buy into people before they buy into ideas. I have bought into Debbie. In this book, Debbie does an amazing job of taking us on her personal and professional journey, sharing her thoughts, her strengths, her fears, and her struggles, before she shares with us her amazing wisdom regarding how we can use technology to make learning stick. As a proponent for Lasting Learning, I think Debbie has nailed it. She has shown us not only why we must evolve as educators, but gives us the tools to do so as well.

Dave Schmittou - Director of Leadership and Development for Teach Better Team- Professor of Educational Leadership at Central Michigan University, Author, Speaker

I don't think I will be able to look at technology and student empowerment the same after reading TRANSFORM. From the moment Debbie brilliantly shared her "why" and purpose in the opening introduction, she captures the essence of what educators are seeking to find. Her anecdotal stories and real-life examples expose her passion for students and how they can be transformed to SHINE when given the opportunity. The journey she communicates to readers is one of twists, turns, and obstacles that led to finding her voice. She invites us to join her in an amazing collaboration full of skillful steps to guide students to expose their full potential.

Jillian DuBois - Elementary Educator,
Author + Illustrator, Tech Tool Enthusiast

Debbie Tannenbaum brings us Transform: Techy Notes to Make Learning Sticky at just the right time. The pandemic has made all educators evaluate their practices in order to reach all students. In Transform, Debbie shares her journey from a resistant user of educational technology to a passionate user and risk taker in order to support her students and colleagues. Debbie shares concrete evidence of the different ways using technology in her classroom has empowered her students and how sharing ideas with her colleagues helps them to grow and learn. You'll read her stories of success but also where she has failed and how she grew and learned from her experiences. Within these pages you will find ideas that you can use as they are or tweak to transform learning in your classroom. This book is a practical guide to "transforming" your classroom through technology

Jay Billy - Proud Principal of Ben Franklin Elementary School, Author

TRANSFORM is an amazing blend of educational anecdotes, instructional tips and tricks, tech tools, and so much more to inspire educational advancement. Through her thoughtful words, author Debbie Tannenbaum takes her reader on a journey toward understanding how to effect meaningful change in the field of education. From the first page to the last page, Debbie not only talks readers through her own experiences, but she recommends many actionable steps for educators to take to lead their classrooms, schools, and districts toward the future of education. As I read her techy notes, Debbie had me realize that "to create a new story of learning, we must change the role of the student and the teacher." After you finish this wonderfully inspiring book, I am confident you will leave more motivated to help with that work.

Dr. Dan Kreiness - Instructional Coach for Digital Learning, Author, Podcaster

Educators around the world are looking for new tools to increase engagement and perpetuate learning in their classrooms. Debbie brilliantly infuses life lessons and technological advances as she takes readers on a journey depicting her tenacity and resolve in the pursuit to becoming a transformational educator. It's awe-inspiring, riveting, while at the same time filled with practical, innovative methods which will help to revolutionize your practice, boost students' digital literacy, and amplify learning in your classroom. Transform: Techy Notes to Make Learning Sticky is a book that all educators should add to their educational toolbox.

Jami Fowler-White - NBCT educator, author,
poet, and CEO of Digital PD 4 You

Using the art of storytelling in Transform: Techy Notes to Make Learning Sticky, Debbie introduces strategies for student engagement and relationship building through the effective use of educational technology and innovative teaching strategies. If you're looking for ready-tested, tried-and-true ways to reinvigorate your classroom, then this book is for you.

Mandy Froehlich - Education Consultant,
Speaker, and Author - Divergent EDU

In, TRANSFORM: Techy Notes to Make Learning Sticky, Debbie walks the reader through her journey as an educator that has had one purpose: Empower students by using technology not as simple tools but as opportunities. Debbie shows how to, "make learning sticky" by encouraging her students to be creative and collaborate with others. The combination of instruction to teachers combined with real-world examples will inspire and motivate the reader to try some of her ideas for themselves! Who would think to use podcasts and videos with third graders? Debbie did! Learn how her self improvement has had a ripple effect on her students and the educators around her. When you pick up Debbie's book, prepare to TRANSFORM yourself into a teacher who makes learning stick!

John VanDusen - U.S. History Teacher, Football Coach, Command and General Staff College Instructor, Author of Lesson 1

A passion for kids and teaching pours out in "Transform" by Debbie Tannenbaum, a must have resource for teachers. Transform is a powerful book with a focus on our why and its importance in education as Debbie shares her journey as an educator. She provides real usable strategies for incorporating technology in the classroom as well as empowering student agency and a focus on making authentic and meaningful connections with our students. A powerful book for all educators today!

Jonathan Alsheimer - Teacher, Speaker, and Author of Next Level Teaching

Unlike professionals who work in the private sector, teachers spend most of the day with children in classrooms. I fully understand they are teaching, and their job is to be in front of students. However, we should be working tirelessly to find new ways for educators to work together when students are not in front of them. I also understand it's tough to find three minutes to use the bathroom, let alone collaborate. But creating opportunities to connect will reduce the feeling of working in a silo.

Debbie Tannenbaum's book TRANSFORM: Techy Notes to Make Learning Sticky used words and ideas to open the metaphorical door to their classroom and world. A teacher can become isolated in their own classroom or academic subject and consequently experiences little to no interaction with colleagues. TRANSFORM: Techy Notes gives an inside look and robust ideas to empower and encourage educators to maximize learning anywhere and anytime.

The book is jam-packed with ideas. Think of a supply room in a school where sticky notes live. That room has a collection of items to support educators. When reading this book, I felt like I was walking into a professional supply room because the book is packed with goodies and practical ideas to support educators' transform.

Dr. Matthew X. Joseph- District Leader and Author

Debbie Tannenbaum is a rock star educator! Her story is inspirational as she poignantly describes how using challenges as opportunities for growth led her to become an expert educator and an innovative tech leader in her field. The tech tips that she shares are excellent and lead readers toward making positive improvements instantly! Reading this book will make you think, wonder, and it will equip you with an arsenal of ideas to make your learning environment much more efficient.

Dr. Brandon Beck - Author of Unlocking Unlimited Potential,
Speaker, Coach, Professor, Consultant

As an Educational Technology leader for over a decade, I loved reading this book. Debbie has done such an amazing job of showing how technology can change instruction, interactions, and the entire classroom experience. By giving insight into her own story, and showing us the wins that have occurred in the classrooms, she gives us an amazing guide to instilling wonderful technology techniques in each classroom. This is a must read for any teacher.

Taylor Armstrong - Chief Information Officer
Hinds Community College

Debbie's book, Transform: Techy Notes to Make Learning Sticky, is an inspirational collection of ideas worth exploring and embedding deeper into our own classroom practices. Debbie provides a great framework for designing programming while fully utilizing technology, from being willing to explore new ways of learning to allowing and setting up for ample student voice and agency in the classroom. Join Debbie Tannenbaum as she tenaciously reminds us of the value that has come from her varied experiences, and the important stories and learning situations that have developed as she has engaged further with her Professional Learning Network. You will not be disappointed with this excellent read, as it provides so many great takeaways to embed in our own teaching practice every single day.

Pawan Wander - Middle School Teacher, Radio Co-Host and
Podcast Co-Host of the Staff Room Podcast

In TRANSFORM: Techy Notes to Make Learning Sticky, Debbie Tannenbaum shares her personal journey with building her professional learning network and her technology skills and provides guidance for teachers to start their own journey. I have long enjoyed reading her blogs and appreciate how much she shares with educators globally. Debbie provides encouragement, inspiration and the right resources to empower educators to make meaningful changes in their teaching practice today. Educators will appreciate Debbie's honesty and vulnerability in sharing her journey. I have followed Debbie's work for several years and highly recommend TRANSFORM: Techy Notes to Make Learning Sticky to any educator looking to improve their teaching practice and enhance the learning opportunities they provide for students. In this book, you will find ideas and inspiration that will empower you to take risks and bring amazing transformations to every classroom every day!

Rachelle Dene Poth - Spanish and STEAM Teacher,
Author, Consultant

Debbie shares an open, honest, and authentic journey through her educational career and transformation that has led her to being a voice in the limitless benefits of incorporating technology into our students' daily lives. While many educators, especially our more "seasoned," may hold fears about embracing technology, Debbie is able to break down how ANY of us can easily begin incorporating more tech within hours and also why we need to for our students' learning and future. Lastly, Debbie expands on the benefits of relying on our crew, our PLN, to get through any obstacle together. I am forever grateful to be a part of hers.

Michael Earnshaw - Principal of Oak Glen Elementary School, Author of
The EduCulture Cookbook: Recipes & Dishes to Positively Transform
Classroom & School Culture, Co-host of Punk Rock Classrooms Podcast

If you're a teacher that wants to go further with technology, then look no further than this book. Debbie Tannenbaum's, Transform: Techy Notes to Make Learning Sticky is exploding with classroom activities, ideas, and tools that you can read about today and apply tomorrow. Debbie's passion for teaching, connected learning, and ultimately students is evident from the very first page of the book. Not only does she share a variety of web tools that are incredible, she provides creative ways to apply them that you know are proven because she's used them with students. Put simply, if you were to put in place the things that Debbie shares, you'll have the tools to maximize your technology in a way that will make learning happen for your students!

Chris Young - Google Innovator and Trainer, TED Master Class Featured Speaker, President of Indiana Connected Educators

Debbie's book is a tech treasure in a sea of books. Not only does her writing tell a tale of a personal journey, but it also provides real examples that could be used right away in your classroom or district. Technology can be used to transform your teaching if the right supports are in place. Transform will have you nodding and taping sticky notes to all surfaces of your computer.

BreAnn Fennell - Ohio Teacher of the Year District 5, Author of Play? Yay!, Play? Yay! Baby Talk and Choose Your Cheer, Teacher Leader Liaison for the State of Ohio, Teach Better Ambassador

TRANSFORM: Techy Notes to Make Learning Sticky is a must read! In this informative, positive, and innovative book, Debbie shares the resources to transform your mindset and instructional practices. If you are ready to spread your technology wings, this book will help you soar! Not only will you gain the tools you need, but you will have the confidence to take risks and break tradition with technology. TRANSFORM: Techy Notes is practical and timely. It includes ideas and strategies you may implement right away. Debbie Tannenbaum has done a fabulous job supporting the education community with her book.

Sari Goldberg McKeown - Elementary Principal

TRANSFORM will encourage and empower teachers. Debbie Tannenbaum paints a picture of what great elementary tech integration could look like -- and then provides concrete steps teachers can take to realize it. All along, she inspires with stories from her own teaching experience, proving that anyone can make big changes.

Matt Miller - Educator, Speaker, Author of Ditch That Textbook

Debbie's journey from struggling as a first-year teacher all of the way to thriving as a technology specialist, author, and connected educator provides an inspirational roadmap for any teacher or leader of teachers. Combine that with examples and stories of elementary technology integrations using more than a dozen tools and tips for growing and leveraging a "PLN" and you've got a book that could TRANSFORM your teaching practice, classroom, and career!

Jake Miller - Author of Educational Duct Tape,
Podcast Host, (@JakeMillerTech)

Debbie Tannenbaum has written a book that every single educator should read-especially as-we enter into a post pandemic society. Debbie shares her journey from flopping to Flipgrid- and the reality that leadership is at the very core of all educational outcomes— for teachers and their students. This book clearly communicates the value and action steps of using tech in the classroom to cultivate creativity and foster risk taking. Hot topics range from PBL and technology (who knew!) to Pear Deck, Padlet, EdPuzzle and Jamboards and the incredible value of PLCs. These platforms have been the topic of every Zoom meeting in the last year! Debbie Tannenbaum's book offers clarity and creativity as we navigate the new normal in education.

Dr. Lori Koerner - Educator, Leader, Author, Fulbright Specialist Scholar

Transform takes educators on a journey that they can relate to. Debbie does a fantastic job of narrowing down key points into digestible bites - creating a simple, yet efficient read. If you're a teacher, you need this book!

Joe and Kristin Merrill - Elementary Teachers,
Authors of the InterACTIVE Class series

Debbie has created an authentic way to view instructional technology that empowers students and educators. Her personal stories of success and failure provide a practical perspective for maximizing the integration of technology into learning experiences that go beyond the basic level of understanding, to grasping the relevance of learning in the world around us. This book is a resource that educators will revisit often as a guide to enhancing instructional technology tools.

Bethany Hill - Consultant, Speaker, Author #JoyfulLeaders

TRANSFORM

Techy Notes to Make Learning Sticky

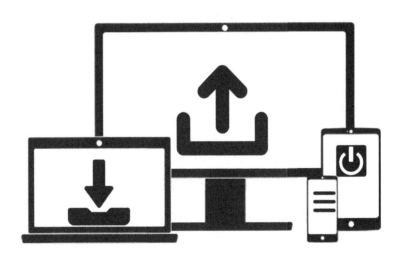

Debbie Tannenbaum

TRANSFORM: Techy Notes to Make Learning Sticky

Copyright © by Debbie Tannenbaum and Darrin M Peppard
First Edition 2021

Road to Awesome, LLC.

Dedication

To my husband, Joe for believing in me before I did, and encouraging me to reach for the stars! It means more to me than I can ever express!

To my children Jacob, Mollie, Josh and Ali for supporting me as I did all "those technology things."

To my PLN for helping me to see a life of abundance that I never could have imagined before.

Acknowledgements

There are so many people that I would like to thank for contributing to this book. All of you are part of my story and I am grateful everyday that our paths intersected and how you added light and joy to my life. I know it will be impossible to include everyone, but I will try to include as many people as I can in the paragraphs that follow.

The first person I want to thank is my husband, Joe. When we first met in 2012, he saw something in me that I didn't know existed, a spark that he inspired me to ignite. When things were tough in my teaching journey, he motivated me to continue on and explore new avenues of education. He is my champion and before I believed in myself, he believed in me. Whether it was presenting more, blogging regularly, or writing this book, he never offered anything but his encouragement and praise. He has been there supporting me every step along the way, even when it added to his to do list. I can't thank him enough, his belief in me was the match that ignited a fire within me that led to all of this.

Next, I need to thank my children, Jacob, Mollie, Josh, and Ali for supporting me in this project. I know there were many times that my book journey took a lot of my time, but you were always gracious and understanding. I am so proud to have such amazing children in my corner.

A very special thanks goes to my publisher, Darrin Peppard. When I contacted you on December 24, 2020, we barely knew each other, but you took a chance on my book, my dream. From our first interactions, you have inspired me and helped me to reach new heights. You believed in my book, my vision so strongly and that propelled me with a passion to finish this book. You have been such an amazing mentor and friend to me through this process. You truly took me on "The Road to Awesome."

To my amazing editor, Jess Peppard, thank you so much for all the hours you spent time editing each of the chapters so thoroughly. The suggestions you provided and clarifying questions you asked improved my book immeasurably. You helped me refine my vision of this book. This book is so much better because of you.

So many people allowed me to share parts of their story in mine. Thank you to:

- Jen Hertzberg, for introducing me to Twitter
- Linda Biberaj, for sharing so many of our co teaching sessions with me.
- Nicole Oberdick, for your innovation in the library and sharing it with me.
- Brittany Long, Brittany Cardenas, and Sharon Powers, for sharing the impact of Twitter on your practice
- Brittany Liberatore, for sharing your awesome Google Slides activities for littles.
- Dawn Reese, for being willing to try new things and share them with others.
- Mike Abrams, for making my first solo presentation a memorable experience.
- Rachelle Dene Poth and Jillian DuBois, for all of your encouragement of my writing and as I went through my book journey.

I also need to thank so many groups included in my Personal Learning Network (PLN)

- The Teach Better Team, especially the support of Rae Hughart and Jeff Gargas
- Teach Better ambassadors, I have learned so much from all of you and all of you inspire me.
- Unlocking Unlimited Potential on the Road to Awesome, for your support and encouragement as I entered uncharted territory. Thanks Brandon Beck and Darrin Peppard for organizing this coaching opportunity.
- Teach Better Administrator Mastermind, the best way to start and end every Tuesday and inspire you all week long.
- Lindsay Titus' Ignite Your Legacy, all of you help me level up every day.

- Leadership Lounge, for some amazing new connections that I can't imagine not having.
- pd4youandme bloggers, for encouraging bloggers to keep writing
- My Clubhouse Edupreneur group, for answering more questions than I knew I had.
- #fcpsSBTS, my crew of School Based Technology Specialists for their support.
- My colleagues and students at Sangster Elementary School, Vienna Elementary School and Flint Hill Elementary School, none of this would have happened without you.

So many other amazing people help to contribute to this accomplishment, it would be impossible to name all of you, but know that I appreciate you so and you are a part of my heart.

Table of Contents

Foreward
Kasey Bell

When I began my teaching career in 2003, like most teachers, I shut my door and taught my students how I was taught--lectures and worksheets. Oh, the lessons we learn as educators! My journey was like many that enter the profession. I loved kids, and I loved school, so I thought that would make me a good teacher. (WRONG!) It's a start, but my journey to transformation as a teacher came when I embraced my own interests in educational technology and discovered new ways to engage my students.

Not unlike Debbie's journey shared in this book, I felt isolated but thought that's how it is supposed to be. I, too, was an early adopter of new technology. I often implemented it in my classroom with little thought as to how it would impact learning. We now call this using technology for technology's sake. I was never really passionate about my content area, English Language Arts, it was just kind of where I ended up. My true passion was edtech.

I quickly realized that I wanted to do more, impact more than just my own students. I wanted to help teachers learn all the "techy tricks." As I pursued my master's degree in educational technology, I really began to see the power that digital tools could have on learning, going beyond what was previously possible. I left my middle school classroom and took a position as an instructional technologist, what would probably be called a tech coach these days. A whole new world of working and collaborating with a team opened up, and through some amazing professional learning opportunities, my mindset shifted.

Some may say I was drinking the Kool-Aid of people like Robert Marzano, John Hattie, and Grant Wiggins. Still, I made connections between research, theory, and the practical application of technology in the classroom. I loved it! I have always loved learning, but in my niche, I couldn't get enough.

Fast forward a few years in my career, and the educational technology landscape was growing and changing rapidly. During my graduate studies, I was introduced to a little web-based word processor called Writely. Today, you know it as Google Docs. (Man, does that make me feel old!) I was hooked immediately. This was a game-changer!

As I learned more about the next big things in technology, I also learned that Google was jumping into the education market. I began learning as much as I could about the suite of tools and discovered Google Certification. I worked hard to become a Google Certified Trainer, which became the turning point of my career. It pushed me to begin blogging, sharing on social media, and connecting with other like-minded educators. Later that same year, I also became a Google Certified Teacher, now referred to as Google Certified Innovator. (Don't miss Debbie's Google Certification journey in chapter 5!)

I share this journey with you not because I'm trying to convince anyone to use Google, but because the program helped me gain new skills and transformed my career. ShakeUpLearning.com wouldn't exist if I didn't push myself. I would have never written a book if I hadn't gotten out of my comfort zone. To truly improve our craft as educators, we must push ourselves--out of our comfort zones and embrace new technologies. That's exactly what this book will help you do!

Debbie shares some fantastic lesson ideas and tools, but y'all know my favorite is her choice boards in chapter four! Voice and choice open so many doors for students. Now, combine that with some awesome tools like Flipgrid and Tinkercad, and you've got a winner! In this choice board, students are given research questions, multiple options to respond, and then get to design their own monument. Students should always be given multiple pathways to learn and create--a perfect way to tap into those 4 C's!

And definitely don't skip out on chapter six, Finding Your PLN! Your personal learning network may quite possibly be the most critical piece to classroom transformation. This book would not exist if Debbie hadn't stepped out and connected with like-minded educators, building a robust PLN.

You may also notice that my name is mentioned quite a bit in this book, which is truly an honor. I love sharing ideas that can inspire teachers in the classroom. That's my greatest joy! We are all better together. Know this, you are not alone. Stop teaching in a silo and connect with educators across the globe.

Throughout this book, you will learn how to use digital tools to transform teaching and learning. The strategies are clear and practical. Use this as your catalyst to get out of YOUR comfort zone and make an impact. Don't ever underestimate what your students are capable of, and always remember to Shake Up Learning!

Introduction

TRANSFORM is an acronym revealing my educational journey. It is not a smooth journey, but it is a real one, full of ups and downs. To survive the roller coaster I needed to know why I did what I did. I needed to find my purpose, my anchor.

I found my purpose working collaboratively with other educators, using technology tools to amplify student learning and empower student voice. To fulfill this work I have dedicated myself to being a lifelong learner, always perfecting my trade.

My passion is not only for my classroom and my school, but my community, ensuring students are using technology in transformative ways to prepare them for the future. I wake up every day excited to do this work. It centers me and keeps me focused, filtering out all the extra noise.

I started my journey full of idealism and ready to save the world. I was greeted by a much different reality. Teaching is hard work and, like any pursuit, requires continual adjustment. Being an educator can be an isolating job, but it doesn't have to be.

TRANSFORM: Techy Notes to Make Learning Sticky, tells the tale of collaborative learning for teachers and students, explaining ways Techy Notes can make learning "sticky" in school. It frames best practices in using technology to provide students with opportunities to learn in new ways and to help that learning stick. You will also learn how to use technology to leverage being a connected educator.

Throughout the book I will reference some amazing people. Their Twitter handles will be in parenthesis. Consider adding them to your professional learning network.

This book is organized in three parts with aspects of the TRANSFORM mindset. Getting Your Feet Wet details the highs and lows of my early years in education and how I learned of the impact of educational technology. Next Steps focuses on student and teacher empowerment and amplifying their voices to the greater educational community. Taking Your Transformation to the Next Level pushes the ideas of teacher empowerment encouraging educators to model their own creation process. As you read I challenge you to find ways to TRANSFORM as an educator.

Thank you for accompanying me on my journey. I hope you will find inspiration and add the TRANSFORM mindset to your educational practice. It has truly changed my life and I know it will transform yours as well.

I would love to hear your stories, too. Feel free to connect with me @TannenbaumTech or using #transform and check out my website and blog at www.tannenbaumtech.com.

After all, we are all better when we work together to TRANSFORM the world around us!

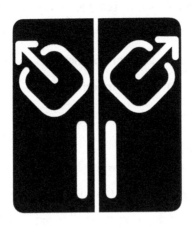

Chapter 1

Turning Away From Teaching Behind Closed Doors

It seems impossible for me to believe I have been in education for over twenty-one years. In many ways I feel like I have only come into my own in the past few years. Before that, my career felt so different, my dreams seemed so far away. Becoming a connected educator helped me reach my dreams.

I was an okay teacher, but now I am a great educator. Becoming a connected educator opened doors, and brought me out of the isolation I felt as a classroom teacher in my earlier years. Back then, it was common practice to just close your door, teach your class, and focus only on your students. Sometimes you might share an idea with a colleague, but team meetings were mostly reserved for school-wide business.

Teaching seemed so different when I started in 1998, but education seems to go in cycles. What is old is new again. What has never changed is my approach to teaching. This past year, I took the Gallup StrengthsFinder test. My top strength was Learner. No surprise there. Even in my early teaching years I would get excited about learning something new.

Becoming a Teacher

I remember as young as eight years old, I wanted to be a teacher. I even made my sister and her friends play school with me. As soon as I was old enough, I started babysitting. When I entered high school, I continued my quest to become a teacher. My parents were against this. My mom went into education in college because she felt this was one of the few things girls could do at that time. She hated it. Still, I persisted. I knew what I wanted.

During high school I immersed myself in experiences related to teaching. After babysitting for many of the young families in my synagogue, I was asked to lead youth services for preschoolers. Teaching *Ketanim*, little ones, was a transformative experience for

4

me. It was there I discovered the creative process involved in education as I planned engaging activities for the students. I watched with delight as abstract religious concepts became more concrete. It was thrilling to become *Morah* Debbie, Teacher Debbie, guide through their service.

I also worked in the summers as a junior counselor at a day camp. During the school year, I had a job at a local day care center after school. I thoroughly enjoyed and knew education was what I was meant to do. In my senior year, I completed an internship with the second grade teacher at my old elementary school. In many ways, I felt like those students were my first class.

After high school, I attended the University of Maryland and majored in elementary education. I continued to work in the education field as I studied. I transferred my *Ketanim* service to Maryland. I rebranded it as *Gesher,* or bridge, for the kindergarten to second grade age group at a local Hebrew school. These services fueled my passion to teach. I left college full of hope and idealism, ready to save the world. Following graduation, I was overjoyed to land an interview with a local school district and ecstatic to be offered a job teaching second grade.

First Year Struggles
My first year teaching was HARD! When I started I was so green, so optimistic and ready to make a difference. I walked into my second

grade classroom thinking it was my dream come true. It gave me so much joy decorating my classroom, getting to know my new colleagues and my seventeen wonderful students.

I quickly learned teaching my own class was very different from any practice experience. In this school there were definite divisions, lots of politics in place. My principal clashed with many of the staff and there was visible tension in the building. As I walked into my interview, I remember the custodian telling me this was not a good place to be. I thought he was joking, but when the first quarter ended and my class grew to twenty-four students in less than two weeks, I realized the truth of his words.

Looking back I am not sure I was fully prepared to start teaching. The school I worked at provided very little support for teachers. Doors were closed between classrooms and we worked in isolation. I was one of two second grade teachers. The other teacher was a veteran teacher who just wanted to teach and stay out of trouble. She did not think I belonged there and did not want to deal with me.

The second quarter continued and things got worse in my classroom. One of my students suffered from an emotional disability and her behavior made instruction increasingly more difficult as the year went on. Her behaviors scared the other students. I was not at all prepared for this. My classroom went from a place of learning to a place of fear. I worried about how I would deal with whatever happened next.

I felt hopeless, waiting anxiously each Friday for the weekend to begin and despondent on Sunday afternoons when it was time to start planning for another long week. To compound my stress, I was living on my own in an apartment for the first time. I was terrified, but I had been raised to never give up. I was determined and believed I could do this.

One afternoon, the principal and assistant principal sat down with me in my classroom. I was told I had two weeks to fix my classroom or leave. When I asked for help, they told me I had already been given more than enough and it was up to me. I didn't know what to do. I was 22 years old and facing one of the hardest decisions in my young life. I loved my students, but I could not do it anymore. The job was making me sick and ruining my passion for teaching.

The day I left that job was one of my saddest moments, one I rarely talk about, much less write about. In fact, as I write this, I still feel the pain of my desperation and despair. I felt like I had failed. It was probably the first time in my life I have ever felt devastated.

Moving On After a Fail

I seriously thought about letting go of my dream to teach. I honestly didn't know what to do. One of my friends suggested substitute teaching and, because I really didn't want to move back home, I gave it a chance. Sometimes you have to take a leap of faith and try again. So, that is what I did.

Rabbi Michael Cohen (@TheTechRabbi) views FAILURE as First Attempt In Learning Unless Reflection Exists. I reflected, and decided to build up and refine my teaching craft. I took a leap and applied for a substitute teaching position in Montgomery County Public Schools.

Teaching in lots of different schools and learning from so many experienced teachers was exactly what I needed. It gave me the chance to start fresh. I really enjoyed substitute teaching and was thrilled when I was offered a long term substitute teaching position for the remainder of the year. I was now part of the staff and things had started to look up.

With renewed confidence and a better state of mind I interviewed for a position at an elementary school. The next school year I started working as a fourth grade teacher in a new school. I was part of a great team and finally found the support I needed.

Discovering Technology's Hidden Talents

It was in the computer lab of this new school that I first discovered the magic of technology. I was astonished by the wealth of activities

8

available on scholastic.com. It gave students authentic purposes for both research and writing.

One of my favorite activities was the Nominate A Trailblazer project. Students read about several influential African American people then selected one to research further using the media center and internet resources. The students detailed why this person should be nominated for the Trailblazer Honor Roll. Students could share their writing on the Scholastic website and see other students' nominations as well.

The students loved it! They were more engaged and invested in their work. When Scholastic hosted Colin Powell as part of a moderated interview at the end of the unit, my students got to submit questions and watch the interview live.

My students were hooked and so was I. These authentic tasks empowered the students and exposed their work to a larger audience. I started looking for other chances to push their learning to a new level. In hindsight, many of these activities were the start of my exploration into Project Based Learning (PBL).

Another activity was linked to our class' read aloud book, Castle In The Attic by Elizabeth Winthrop (1985). Students were asked to determine whether or not the castles in the book were authentic and to summarize their final thoughts in a letter to Kidsworld magazine. As we read this book, students used both print and online resources to research this subject. I was surprised by their growth and how much this activity had activated their learning.

Seeing the creativity technology brought to my classroom inspired me to get my Master's Degree in Technology for Educators from Johns Hopkins University. This was where I first began to find the community I had been looking for, like minded individuals who were as passionate about using technology to improve instruction as I was.

After completing my Master's degree and becoming a new mom, I continued working as a classroom teacher. I taught fourth grade, one of my favorites, and middle school, definitely not my cup of tea. These experiences led me to become more confident and ready to take a new step.

Becoming a Technology Teacher

After teaching for a few years, an exciting opportunity presented itself, a part-time position as a technology teacher came open. I was able to collaborate with teams on a regular basis designing design lessons and activities using technology to support the curriculum. We co-taught the lessons in the computer lab. Watching my colleagues learn alongside their students was such a joy.

As part of the school leadership team, I not only led our school's technology committee, but also professional development sessions. The school improvement plan focused on supporting English Language Learners using technology tools. I provided training on ways technology could enrich instruction using tools like screen reader, adaptive technology and visual scaffolding to improve instruction and facilitate learning.

Returning to the Classroom

I now had two children and had gone through a divorce. I needed a steady full-time job. When I returned to the classroom things were changing. Teams were starting to plan collaboratively. I joined a Primary Years Program (PYP) International Baccalaureate faculty, which I thoroughly enjoyed. We worked together to plan our units and had just started using Promethean boards. I was excited by the possibilities they brought educators.

The I to I Classroom

A couple of years later, I remarried and moved to Virginia. I continued teaching in the same county, now as a fifth grade teacher. Before my second year at the school, my principal wanted to know if I would be interested in being the team leader for fifth grade. The school was getting ready to move to a I to I classroom and, based on my technology background, she was counting on my experience to help us make the transition.

A colleague and I created an orientation plan which had several components. This plan was extremely successful for several reasons. First, it helped teachers and other staff learn how to organize and manage student technology use in the classroom. Second, it provided students with clear routines and expectations when using technology. Last, it informed the parent community of these expectations. Two colleagues were a little resistant to this change. However, the implementation plan eased their concerns and enabled them to be technology leaders in their classroom.

This was my first experience with a 1 to 1 environment. Google tools enabled my students to collaborate and create. As we departmentalized, I was able to work with my colleagues to plan for our students.

Another Challenge

After three years of commuting, I determined I was spending way too much time in transit. I decided to look for a job closer to home. I found a spot teaching fourth grade in a small district. It was definitely a culture shock for me, but I was excited for this new opportunity. Unfortunately, like my first year teaching, what looks good initially can be very different day to day.

For most of my career, I had taught in large school systems. This small system was not a good fit for me. The administrators had set up an environment that thrived on staff apprehension. Flying under the radar was considered the best course of action there. My colleagues were supportive, but the constant pressure from this administration was unyielding. I felt as if I couldn't do anything right. For the second time in my teaching career, I doubted my ability and thought about leaving teaching. Luckily for me, my husband would not let me give up. The following year I started working in Fairfax County Public Schools, Virginia.

Joining a Connected Learning Environment

I first heard about Twitter when I joined the Fairfax County Public Schools (FCPS) family. My school was promoting Twitter so I joined. Working in a connected school changed everything by enabling me to have a professional learning network (PLN) from which to learn and grow.

My principal, Jen Hertzberg (@tchrwithatitle), was a connected learner who embraced the learner mindset. She was always learning and pushed her staff to do the same. I learned a lot that year. She introduced our staff to Project Zero's Thinking Routines, we were immersed in Project Based Learning and we learned how to use collaborative learning teams to plan for instruction.

China Museum

One of my favorite memories from that year was our China PBL unit. My class investigated how the contributions and accomplishments of Ancient China influenced the development of the culture and why they are still relevant today. This project dug into the ways the modern day world is affected by the past.

This project was an extensive undertaking. Students were asked to assume the role of a museum curator and create an interactive museum exhibit to educate others about the importance of Ancient China. We used technology to explore similar exhibits and Vimeo to watch a Kid Curators video to build background knowledge. We wanted the students to think big and go beyond traditional tri-fold board displays.

I introduced my class to Google Classroom to share a variety of resources that were essential to this unit. We were researchers and learning information for an authentic purpose. We used tools just as a curator would, building our depth of knowledge then creating interactive exhibits.

Early on, we used a variety of databases to help us write comprehensive, researchable questions. This allowed students to reach beyond the school's library and access a wealth of materials and information. I encouraged the students to use these as a primary source of reference material.

During the creation of exhibits, students used a variety of technology. Quizizz was used to create surveys and quizzes on the exhibits. Google Slides was used to display results. Students typed scripts and used iPads to create videos for their exhibits.

As all educators should do, we began with the end in mind. From day one, students had access to the PBL rubric on Google Classroom. In addition, I used Google Forms surveys to check in weekly with my students on their progress. I specifically focused on Portrait of a Graduate skills in these check-ins.

Proof of success was there on Museum Day! As students presented their projects, I used my class Twitter account to live stream their exhibits to a wider audience. Parents and staff continually complimented the exhibits. Afterwards, one parent posted, "What an amazing Chinese Museum! I was blown away by the outstanding exhibits. Nice job!!"

With all of my new learning and connections, I found myself taking more risks. My principal and the school's technology specialist encouraged me, leading me to apply for a school-based technology specialist position. I was beside myself when I received the email informing me I had made it into the pool of potential candidates. I believe I screamed loud enough for everyone in the school to hear me when I was granted an interview.

The past couple of years had been the best years of my career to that point. I was working my dream job with students and teachers. I was using technology to enhance instruction and provide new opportunities. I woke up every day excited to share my zeal for using educational technology. I believed, after surviving challenges and setbacks, I had finally discovered my true calling.

Share how turning away from closed doors changed your journey using #transform.

Chapter 2

Revisiting Technology's role in Education

Among the many books I have read related to technology and instruction, Shake Up Learning: Practice Ideas to Move from Static to Dynamic by Kasey Bell (2018) might be the most impactful. As she describes in the forward, she spoke a language I not only understood but was seeking in my practice. The tagline for her book quickly became my mantra, "Technology is not just a tool, but it is an opportunity."

Using technology is not just about the tools in and of themselves, but the opportunities they provide students. Our students are growing up in a very different world from us. Finding information is not their challenge, information is literally at their fingertips. Their challenge is to determine if the information is reliable, how they should use it and how it can best be synthesized.

Many educators worry students will struggle to find the balance between using technology tools and applying information gained from these tools. They fear it will take too long to teach their students how to use the technology and how to manage students in the process. Fear not! We will go over strategies to ease these fears later in chapter four. We need to reveal the uses these technology tools have and how they affect the learning experience.

Many technology integration models address the implementation of technology in education: Technological, Pedagogical, and Content Knowledge (TPACK) and Substitution, Augmentation, Modification, Redefinition (SAMR) to name two. What all these models have in common is how the educator chooses to use the technology in their classrooms. As a technology coach, my goal is to always use technology to amplify the learning experience and allow the learner to do something that would not have been possible otherwise.

It can be easy to get overwhelmed by the variety of available educational technology applications. Below are my top ten picks in my TRANSFORM Tech Toolkit. To be considered as a TRANSFORM tool, they first need to provide opportunities not possible without the technology. In addition, they can be used in any setting, any subject, and with any age group. Some of these I use more often than others, but they are all terrific. Regardless of how often I use them, they transform or enhance the learning experience.

#1 Flipgrid

What opportunities does it provide students?

Flipgrid is an asynchronous and engaging video discussion board in which students can respond to each other in a manner of their choosing. They can respond with just video or audio, and they can add stickers or custom graphics of their own. Students can even record their screens to use as a response.

Teachers can set up prompts or choose from already created topics in the Discovery Library. They can decide what permissions to grant their students and customize the responses they can give. It is an awesome tool and even more important, it is FREE!

How does it transform the learning experience?

The video based discussion board allows students to demonstrate their thinking anywhere, anytime. Flipgrid is not only versatile, it allows for student to student interactions, something all students need in our current educational settings.

Getting started:

Teachers will set up individual topics or groups. Groups are like binders and contain many topics. Teachers then send a link to their students to log into the topic. From there, students can respond to the teacher's prompt using a variety of options.

Want to learn more? Check out Using Flipgrid to Connect with Students Learning Opportunity using the QR code at the end of this chapter.

What it pairs best with:

Flipgrid is a great tool to use when you want to display student thinking. Because of this, I often use it to amplify Thinking Routines, which I will discuss in chapter three. Flipgrid also works well with empowering student voice, which we will learn more about in chapter four.

See it in action:

When I first learned about Flipgrid, I was definitely skeptical. I held off trying it at first until one of my colleagues used it in some of her lessons. I began to see the power of this tool, so I started off small by using Flipgrid towards the end of the year.

Using a template of a Tic Tac Toe Choice Board from Kasey Bell's book, I added a square for Flipgrid to allow students to make book reviews. Over half of my students chose this square. It was helpful for students to hear their reflections. It allowed them to listen to each other and have an archive of favorite books in my class.

#2 Google Slides

What opportunities does it provide students?
Google Slides has many capabilities every educator should know about. Yes, it can be used as a presentation tool, but it can do so much more. Students are afforded marvelous opportunities when using Google Slides. Being a collaborative tool, many students can work together in one Slide Deck. This is a wonderful way to give students agency while encouraging collaboration. One of my classes used Gale Elementary's Kids InfoBits (Gale, n.d.) allowing students to take collaborative notes about the American Revolution. Another class took collaborative notes on their project about Oceans.

How does it transform the learning experience?
Theresa Wills, a professor at George Mason University, has shared her interactive Slides with many educators. Through Slides her students interact with content in a Slide Deck all can edit. Professor

Wills' website, http://www.theresawills.com, and her book, Teaching Math at a Distance (2020), outline innovative ideas to make synchronous online instruction more interactive.

Another feature is the ability to link to other Slides. I used this when my students made Choose Your Own Adventure story books. They could link their story options to other Slides to continue the story. Another group of students used this same feature to create a simulated app experience that addressed a need in our school. Because Google Slides integrates with YouTube, you can add videos directly into the Slides and even crop the section you want students to focus on.

Getting started:

The easiest way to start a Slide Deck is to type slides.new into your internet browser. From there, you can begin to add Slides to your Slide Deck.

Check out the QR code at the end of the chapter if you want to learn more with my Google Slides Basics Learning Opportunity.

What it pairs best with:

Google Slides works well anytime you want your students to work collaboratively or see each other's thinking. It lends itself well in exhibiting Thinking Routines (Ch. 3). In addition, because of its linking abilities, it also works great with HyperDocs and Choice Boards (Ch. 4)

See it in action:

One of my teachers is a master at using Google Slides. She created a template of different graphics students could choose from to create valentines for their classmates. She has also created similar templates for treasure maps and gingerbread decoration. Each student receives their own Slide, but can also see other students' Slides as well.

#3 Pear Deck

What opportunities does it provide?

Pear Deck redefines instruction. It makes any Google Slides presentation interactive using a variety of different slide types including: multiple choice, text, number, website, drawing, and draggable. Using these Slide formats, students have the opportunity to demonstrate their thinking. Teachers can not only give feedback to students in real time, but display student work anonymously to validate student thinking as a class.

How does it transform the learning experience?

Whether students are learning face to face, virtual, or hybrid, Pear Deck makes their learning interactive. Even my youngest learners have used it. One of my first grade teachers really enjoys using Pear Deck for assessments. She appreciates how it compels the students to stay with her on each question. With student names at the bottom of the screen, she knows who has not started their Slide yet. This allows her to prompt the student to keep moving and prevents her from returning to a question for just one student.

One of my teachers likes the data she can get from Pear Deck. She also appreciates that students and parents can look at what is written or drawn on each Slide. It helps deepen the students' understanding and allows the teacher to see who may be struggling. Students are held accountable for doing the work because she can see who is responding and who is not.

Getting started:

You can use Pear Deck with any Google Slide Deck. All you need to do is download the add-on from the Chrome store or download the Pear Deck Power Up Extension. You can choose and adjust templates or make your own. You can also add interactive questions to them.

Once the deck is ready, click Start Lesson and choose from Instructor Paced (synchronous) or Student Paced modes (asynchronous). The teacher can control the pace, if they want, and add feedback as their students work. You can even add another teacher to the session. Teachers share the sessions using a link and each student can log in using their Google or Microsoft credentials.

After the lesson is over, teachers can create student takeaways for student feedback that goes directly to the Google Drive.

To learn more, check out Powering Up Learning with Pear Deck using the QR code at the end of this chapter.

What it pairs best with:

Pear Deck works well when you want to hear from all students. Many teachers use it for math and sharing mathematical thinking. It also works well with Thinking Routines (Ch. 3) and is a great way to empower student voice (Ch. 4).

See it in action:

Our school's librarian, Nicole Oberdick (@MrsOberdick), used Pear Deck for class read-aloud lessons. It was a fantastic way for students to clearly see the pictures in the books and engage with the story. Students could interact with the text and illustrations as well as display their thinking and questions as they read together. The librarian tried to incorporate at least one of each type of Pear Deck Slide (text, drawing, draggable, etc.) in each lesson to differentiate and keep it interesting. If she wanted to make a lesson asynchronous, she utilized the audio feature and recorded the story text on each slide. She appreciated the ability to share a spreadsheet with classroom teachers for formative assessment and participation tracking purposes.

#4 Wixie

What opportunities does it provide students?

Wixie is a user-friendly creation tool. Its user interface includes easy to recognize icons to help students develop icon literacy. They also have an outstanding royalty-free collection of stickers and graphics.

You will appreciate Wixie because of its excellent teacher dashboard to easily manage and review student work. Wixie also has a cloning option allowing you to make infinite copies of a graphic. This is great when students create using shapes, money, etc.

How does it transform the learning experience?

Wixie, like Google Slides, is a fantastic creation tool for students in elementary school. Its easy interface combined with royalty free images, photographs and sounds make it a great way for students to communicate their learning. Like Google Slides, it also allows collaboration and video can be added into your projects.

Wixie is an all inclusive program allowing students to work with video, audio, and clipart in one easy to use program. With options like cloning items, it also works well with math and other hands-on subjects.

Getting started:

Wixie allows you to log in with both Google and Clever. Once students log in, they can work on a preassigned template created by the teacher or start a new project.

Want to learn more about using Wixie? Check out my Wonderful Ways to Use Wixie Learning Opportunity with the QR code at the end of the chapter.

What it pairs best with:

Wixie works best when encouraging student creation. Students can use paint tools, shapes, images, audio and video.

See it in action:

For a while now, January has been my favorite time to work with kindergarten students. After several months of hard work, this is the time when my littlest learners transition from consuming digital content to creating it. This milestone requires a lot of collaboration. Classroom teachers encourage students to practice. Paraprofessionals work with students both in their classroom and during technology classes. Parents help their children learn logins and passwords. Continual repetition is needed on all fronts, but in January, the students are finally ready.

The day we started to create using Wixie, we first reviewed the icons they already knew. Then, we reviewed how to log in. Once they were in, they began to create by adding two stickers to their snow globes.

Their joy and excitement as they learned these simple tasks was contagious. As they worked, I took out my phone to take photos. They were so proud and immediately agreed to have their pictures tweeted out when I asked.

The following week, these students used paint tools to add colors to their projects. The last week in January, they added text and recorded their voices. It was remarkable watching our littlest learners build these skills one by one.

Using Wixie has made this process much more accessible for my kindergarten students. This program scaffolds the creation experience for our younger students and gives them ways to create with a variety of media.

#5 Padlet

What opportunities does it provide students?

Padlet is essentially a digital bulletin board that has many different formats. These allow students to not only see each other's work, but to respond to each other, given the correct permission set.

Unlike other programs, Padlet allows any number of people to participate in these collaborations. It is easy to use and embraces the principles of Universal Design for Learning (CAST, 2018) in its many response options. Students can choose to write, create an audio recording, make a video, and so much more.

How does it transform the learning experience?

Padlet provides opportunities for students in its versatility. Students can create an interactive timeline or create a mock social media stream. The Wall feature can create a virtual bulletin board or you could scaffold questions with the Shelf feature.

Getting Started:

Go to the Padlet website and log in using your Google, Facebook or Microsoft credentials. Once you have logged in, you can choose from eight different templates, based on your needs.

To learn more about Padlet, check out the learning opportunity with the QR code at the end of the chapter.

What it pairs best with:

Padlet works well anytime you want students to work collaboratively or benefit from seeing each other's ideas. It works great with Thinking Routines (Ch. 3). It also allows students to like and comment on each other's work if you choose those options.

See it in action:

During my STEAM classes, students often participated in design challenges. After they finished, students used Padlet to share their creations by taking a picture or screenshot. Each grade level had a Padlet created for this purpose so every student could share their work with others.

#6 Smithsonian Learning Lab

What opportunities does it provide students?

The Smithsonian Learning Lab put all of the Smithsonian's museum collections at your fingertips. On their website, https://learninglab.si.edu/, you have the ability to search any topic by age, subject, etc., allowing you to interact with artifacts from anywhere.

Teachers can either review already curated learning lab collections and edit them or create their own. Students can zoom in and look at these exhibits in ways they can't in real life. They can see artifacts based on topic, not just location.

How does it transform the learning experience?

The Smithsonian Learning Lab brings the magic of any Smithsonian museum to your device.

How to use:

Using the Smithsonian Learning Lab is easy. Just go to the website and search using the magnifying glass. Click on the Learning Lab resource when it pops up. You will probably be overwhelmed by the results, so consider refining and updating your search using subject and age range.

Check out their Basics Guide using the QR code at the end of the chapter.

What it pairs best with:

This works well anytime teachers want students to review artifacts and/or primary resources and it works particularly well with the Thinking Routine See, Think, Wonder.

See it in action:

I asked Ms. Biberaj's students which of them had visited a museum recently. Almost all of the students raised their hands. I then asked how they got to the museum. Students shared modes of transportation including car, metro, airplane, bus, and even Uber. "What if I said you could visit a museum right here in your classroom," I continued. The students looked at me with questioning eyes. I then explained the Smithsonian Museum had digitized its collection and we were going to look at one small collection of artifacts using the Smithsonian Learning Lab to learn about Jamestown. Next, I announced that each of them would select just one artifact and use a Thinking Routine called See, Think, Wonder to analyze this resource.

Students logged in and entered the collection I had curated. Students learned the power of zooming in to see details. They first made observations, then inferences and finally, asked questions. The students were so engaged! As their teacher and I walked around the classroom, the conversations we had with the students were fantastic. We really got to discuss and interpret these primary resources.

It warmed my heart to see this email from Ms. Biberaj (@msbiberaj), "What an exciting opportunity for our students to take a closer look at primary sources. You essentially created a Jamestown exhibit that we got to explore virtually. The kids were all engaged as they used the See-Think-Wonder thinking routine! I am looking forward to embedding the resources in future lessons!"

Technology can transform learning. Without sharing these resources with students and teachers, this experience would never have been possible on a Tuesday morning in a portable classroom.

#7 Pear Deck's Flashcard Factory

What opportunities does it provide students?

Pear Deck's Flashcard Factory is an amazing tool many people may not know about. It allows students to create collaborative flashcards. This program works well in any setting, such as classrooms and remotely in breakout rooms. You can use this for any subject area, even math

How does it transform the learning experience?

Students work collaboratively to create word problems or sentences with matching illustrations. To do this students need to listen, ask questions, and share their ideas. In addition, they are able to create unique solutions with their own voice. Each team has the same problems, yet the solutions on their cards are all very different. Students also ask questions to clarify, explore, and assess ideas as they work on their flashcards.

After all the flashcards are made students begin quality control. They discuss the cards and determine whether or not they are good examples. All approved flashcards can either be shared as a PDF or exported for use in Gimkit.

Getting Started:

Getting started is super easy. Go to peardeck.com and choose Pear Deck vocabulary. You will see a form you can fill out with terms and definitions. Just a note here, sometimes I don't include definitions when I use this with math. After all the terms are filled in and you are ready to use the flashcards, click Play Flashcard Factory and your students will be given a code to join. Once all students have joined, Pear Deck will randomly partner them and decide whether they are part of the Day or Night shift. Students find their partner and get started.

If you want to learn more, check out Fire Up Learning with Flashcard Factory using the QR code at the end of the chapter.

What it pairs best with:

Flashcard Factory works well with any vocabulary work and explaining important events or terms. I really like using it for math. I give students math problems as terms and ask them to draw a solution and write a word problem to match the math problem.

See it in action:

My first experience with this program was with a class studying Caesar's English. The teacher and I decided Flashcard Factory was a good way to practice their words. As we began the activity, I was not sure exactly how this would work. I had used it in a training session, but I was totally unprepared for the experience I was about to have. It was a huge success. Watching the students as they engaged with the content was captivating. They were not only using their knowledge of the words, but were collaborating as they created cards. Moreover, as we reached the quality control portion of the lesson, the discussions we had about each of their proposed cards engaged all students.

#8 Adobe Spark

What opportunities does it provide students?

Adobe Spark has three components: Post, Video, and Page. One of the things I enjoy is how easy this program is to use. If you click it, you can change it. Students have access to all sorts of media within the program. They can easily create videos, graphics and even webpages. Even more impressive is how professional their products look!

How does it transform the learning experience?

Adobe Spark gives students of all ages easy access to an amazing suite of tools. With a simple click of the mouse, students can create videos using images, voiceovers, music and more. They can also create impressive webpages and graphics using these tools as well.

Getting started:

Using Adobe Spark for Education is fairly easy. Just go to https:// spark.adobe.com/sp/login and log in as a teacher or student using either your Google, Facebook or Apple credentials. Click the blue plus sign to get started and choose from a wide variety of projects.

From there, you can use a template (they have lots) or create your own.

What it pairs best with:

Adobe Spark works well with all platforms. You can use it in Flipgrid to download projects and use them wherever you want.

See it in action:

We used Adobe Spark's Video to create museum exhibits about the American Revolution and film trailers to convince others to visit these exhibits. Some of my students used Adobe Spark to create illustrated picture books with their vocabulary for a science unit. Some students even used it to explain their math reasoning while solving problems.

#9 EdPuzzle

What opportunities does it provide students?

Using EdPuzzle is a great way to flip instruction. I have also used it in Choice Boards and HyperDocs, which are discussed in chapter four, to provide accountability for watching videos.

How does it transform the learning experience?

It is no secret our students have a predilection for watching YouTube. Edpuzzle capitalizes on this and can turn any video into an interactive experience. There are many options available in how it can be used. Search tons of pre-made videos or make your own. Add in multiple choice and open ended questions. As a teacher you can check on your students' progress and use this data formatively. In addition, EdPuzzle has video editing tools to crop videos and even add your voice and notes.

Getting Started:

Go to www.edpuzzle.com and choose whether you are a teacher or student. Log in with Google to get started. From there, you have two choices. You can search to find lessons that have already been used in edPuzzle or add your own content to the site. EdPuzzle allows you to edit videos by adding voice overs, multiple choice questions and notes.

Want to learn more? Check out the EdPuzzle Learning Opportunity using the QR code at the end of the chapter.

What it pairs best with:

EdPuzzle can be used with any lesson containing video content. You can upload a video you use regularly to the site. Any time you want formative data and students can watch a video, EdPuzzle is the tool for you!

See it in action:

During a Project Based Learning unit on Oceans, students watched two videos on the impact of plastics on the complex systems of the oceans. I put these videos in EdPuzzle so I could check for individual understanding of the topics discussed.

I have even used EdPuzzle for asynchronous professional development. I uploaded the videos of synchronous training to EdPuzzle and added questions throughout the video. This allowed my colleagues to receive professional development credit they could complete anywhere, anytime.

#10 Google Forms

What opportunities does it provide?

Google Forms is a great way to check in with students. It allows you to gather formative data that easily converts into a Google Sheet. With Forms you can easily add videos, pictures and even your voice inside a Form. Plus, using the branching features, you can create responsive assessments.

How does it transform the learning experience?

Google Forms provides educators innovative ways to collect information from their students. In doing so, this application amplifies student voices. It also integrates with Google Sheets, making it easy to analyze the resulting data.

Getting Started:

Type forms.new into your internet browser to get started. You can also access Forms from your Google Drive. Once you open a Form, you have many choices for customization and themes. If you decide to use it as a quiz there are many question types to choose from: short answer, paragraph, multiple choice, check boxes and more. Want to learn more about making Google Forms? Check out the QR code at the end of the chapter.

What it pairs best with:

Google Forms pairs well with almost any assignment. It allows you to add voice recordings, videos and graphics to help all of your students access the content. It can be used in both summative and formative methods.

See it in action:

One of my favorite ways to use Google Forms is in the classroom as a check-in. I often have a Google Form ready for students to complete when they arrive or begin a class to update me on their current progress and any questions they might have. Another great use would be to collect data from your school's or class' families. Using conditional formatting, you can set Google Forms to only accept certain answers, which is great for breakouts..

These examples are just the tip of the iceberg in how technology can give our students new opportunities. By revisiting technology's role in education, we can audit our current uses to see where we can integrate technology in new and innovative ways.

Share ways you give students opportunities through technology using #transform.

Chapter 3
Amplifying Learning Using Technology Tools

In what ways are your students using technology in class? Are they sitting in front of a computer going 'drill and kill' exercises as they practice math facts or is technology used by them to share their thinking with an audience? One way will build compliance and short term achievement as they consume learning, while the other allows students to synthesize their learning and make it their own. I am sure you know where I stand on this issue. I wholeheartedly believe all of our students should use their voice and choice to create products.

Some might say there isn't enough time to create with all the curriculum educators need to cover. Some might say their students are behind and need to catch up. However, these sprints will lead to short term gains and exhaustion. How can we find time to create and what role does technology play?

Many times we think of creation as a big, involved process that will take days, weeks, maybe months. This is not the case. According to the Merriam-Webster dictionary (n.d.), to create means "to bring [something] into existence," or "to produce through imaginative skill." So, anything we ask students to do fits under this definition. Maybe we should view creation through a different lens and realize technology provides us a multitude of ways to display our creations.

Creating with Thinking Routines

When my administration first introduced the staff to Thinking Routines, I thought they were just glorified graphic organizers. This was not the case. Thinking Routines take what the student has read or learned and scaffolds their thinking with deliberate steps. This helps them reach the targeted thinking needed to move students from consuming to creating by presenting their ideas in a visible manner.

There are many Thinking Routines, all with a different purpose. Some facilitate understanding and creativity, while others focus on fairness and truth. In the past few years, Project Zero's Thinking Routines Toolbox containing these structures has grown exponentially. On their own, they are powerhouses, providing structures to help reveal student thinking. When we amplify these Thinking Routines using technology tools, we provide our students with ways to think better and display their thinking. There are a variety of programs to promote our students' voices making them perfect partners for Thinking Routines. To get you started I have highlighted my six favorite programs.

#1 Padlet

Why use this tool for Thinking Routines?
As described in the second chapter, Padlet is a virtual wall where students can post ideas and thoughts with the rest of their learning community in a safe forum. Padlet has a variety of formats to do this.

How can I use this tool with Thinking Routines?
The Shelf format is ideal for Thinking Routines such as See, Think, Wonder. My students used Padlet to examine artifacts in the Smithsonian Learning Lab from ancient Egypt. Each student had the chance to describe what they saw while viewing the artifact, what they thought the story behind the artifact was, and what they wondered about the artifact.

What do you SEE when you look at this artifact?	What do you THINK the story is behind this artifact?	What do you WONDER about this artifact?
the blue thing looks like a rusty trumpet that was covered by brown freckles	an ancient thing that someone found on the ground a long time ago	I wonder who made it and where it was made. I wonder where it was found.
I see a stone statue man or king	I think people made the statue to respect the king.	I wonder who the statue is. Is the man a symbol of freedom?

Not only did they get to demonstrate their own thinking, but students also saw their classmates' thoughts as well. Using these columns helped students focus on one aspect of the Thinking Routine at a time, while the entire Padlet acted as a record of the group's thoughts.

The Stream feature creates a mock social media feed where students can post, plus they can react and respond to classmates' posts. This format works well with the Headlines Thinking Routine, which asks students to create a headline encapsulating the main idea of what they have learned. My students used this strategy after watching two EdPuzzle videos on the impact of plastics in the ocean. Students collaboratively created headlines then were able to see their classmates' headlines too.

The Wall feature acts like a bulletin board using the Color, Symbol, Image Thinking Routine. Students identify a color, a symbol, and an image to represent their understanding of a topic, then explain their choices. My students used this format to show what they had learned about using digital images correctly. They had fun seeing and commenting on each other's choices.

#2 Pear Deck

Why use this tool for Thinking Routines?

As I discussed in the previous chapter I am very fond of Pear Deck. It takes any Google Slides presentation and makes it interactive using a variety of different Slide types. Students share their thinking and teachers can not only give feedback in real time, but also display work anonymously to validate student thinking as a class.

How can I use this tool with Thinking Routines?

One of my favorite uses of Pear Deck is Drawing Slides. This allows students to demonstrate their thoughts with words or pictures. This works really well with the I Used to Think…Now I Think Thinking Routine. Every student gets a chance to display their thinking and teachers provide students with both choice and voice in how they express their responses. This works for almost any topic, subject and age. Students can choose to respond with text or draw, as illustrated in the example below.

I used to think...	Now I think...
?	Want to dig in

The Draggable Slide, in combination with the Text Slide, is ideal for the Tug of War Thinking Routine, in which students determine where they stand on an issue. In a classroom environment, this allows students to select their stance and not be persuaded otherwise by a peer. The student drags the icon along the rope to where they stand on the topic. The Text Slide then gives each student the chance to express why they selected this particular location on the rope.

Stance #1   Place your flag by where you stand   Stance #2

#3 Flipgrid

Why use this tool for Thinking Routines?

Students can create a video using many options such as a whiteboard, blackboard, or screen recording features. Words and stickers can also be added to compliment the videos. Students can also comment on other's videos and respond to comments about their own videos.

How can I use this tool with Thinking Routines?

One of my classes used the Thinking Routine Circle of Viewpoints to analyze the Declaration of Independence. Each student created a short video from the viewpoint of a British soldier, female colonist, or slave and shared their perspective on the Declaration of Independence. Not only did this help students to better understand the impact of the Declaration of Independence, but allowed them to develop a culturally responsive mindset.

My kindergarten students used Flipgrid for the Think, Puzzle, Explore Thinking Routine. Each student created a short video sharing what they thought about when they saw an American flag, what questions they had about the flag, and how they could learn more about our flag.

#4 Google Slides

Why use this tool for Thinking Routines?

Google Slides allows students to work collaboratively inside of one Slide Deck. This makes it a great choice to pair with many Thinking Routines.

How can I use this tool with Thinking Routines?

I used the Thinking Routine Connect, Extend, Challenge while researching the American Revolution using a database of articles. Each student was assigned one Slide to record their connection to these articles, how these articles extended what they knew, and any lingering questions regarding the article.

Article Citation	How does this CONNECT to what I already know?	How does this EXTEND what I know?	What CHALLENGES me about what I read?
"Native Americans." *Kids InfoBits*, Gale, a Cengage Company, 2018. *Kids InfoBits*, https://link.gale.com/apps/doc/MMIEQN822291118/ITKE?u=fairfaxcps&sid=ITKE&xid=29fd749a. Accessed 5 Feb. 2020.	The Native Americans came from the continent of Asia 14,000 years ago. In that time, dry land connected Asia and North America. Native Americans settled in the North and hunted animals for food.	I learned that native Americans were the first people to live in North America and that the natives would travel to find the animals to eat.	They said that the Europeans were friendly to the natives but then they said they were not so friendly but why could they not just separate the land instead of taking it away from the natives?

#5 Synchronous Chats

Why use this tool for Thinking Routines?

In March of 2020 the education world changed. The COVID-19 pandemic forced educational institutions around the world into remote learning. Students went from face to face connections to listening to a screen. Teachers wanted to improve both engagement and attention. This was easier said than done. Thinking Routines combined with synchronous chats offer ways to amplify learning. Whether your school used Zoom, Google Meet, Blackboard Collaborate Ultra or Teams, all of these synchronous programs have a chat feature. Students who are hesitant to show their faces or speak out loud are far more likely to share in a chat. Here are two Thinking Routines that pair well with these chats.

How can I use this tool with Thinking Routines?

In Take Note, a student chooses one of four questions. Then they label their answer in the chat as Important Point, Something that Puzzles Them, Questions They Still Have, or Something Interesting.

The 4 C's also gives students a choice of four prompts focused on determining Connections, Challenges, important Concepts and Changes in thinking. Students come up with a variety of responses to show their learning to the entire class while providing the teacher great formative data. Student responses create a chat waterfall full of great ideas from which all can learn.

#6 Jamboard

Why use this tool for Thinking Routines?

The collective nature of Jamboard makes it one of my favorite ways to amplify Thinking Routines. Jamboard is powerful in breakout sessions when you set your own backgrounds. Each group has their own frame, but can still work collaboratively. It is easy to use sticky notes as well as the pen and shape tools.

How can I use this tool with Thinking Routines?

Compass Points is a fantastic Thinking Routine for synthesizing ideas. Grade level staff teams used this Routine in breakout groups to process their feelings about returning to school after remote learning. In their groups, they answered the following questions:

Need to Know: What else do you need to know or find out about this idea or proposition? What additional information would help you to evaluate things?

Stance or Suggestion for Moving Forward: What is your current stance or opinion on the idea or proposition? How might you move forward in your evaluation of this idea or proposition?

Excited: What excites you about this idea or proposition? What is the upside?

Worrisome: What do you find worrisome about this idea or proposition? What is the downside?

50

Take Note provides your class opportunities to reflect and synthesize ideas. I used Take Note as a way to summarize during my session about Amplifying Thinking Routines Using Technology Tools. In this example, participants got to choose one of four questions to reflect upon. What is the most important part? What do you find challenging, puzzling, or difficult to understand? What questions would you like to discuss? What is something you found interesting? Students could respond to at least one question on a sticky note and move it to the appropriate corner. This is a great way to reflect as a group.

Thinking Routines partnered with technology tools amplifies not only your students' thinking, but the impact of the Routines themselves. Technology's greatest gift is to provide students with new and unique opportunities. Help your students think better and give these partnerships a try.

Digging Deeper into How Technology Can Amplify Creativity

Why focus on creativity?

Since getting my Master's Degree in Technology for Educators over eighteen years ago, I have been promoting the idea of creating over consuming content. I use technology to provide my students with opportunities to create in new and innovative ways. The tools might have advanced and changed, but the ideas and pedagogy behind them have not.

When I got an opportunity to attend the Adobe Creative Educator Day, I could never have imagined what a life changing experience it would be. This was an entire day dedicated to promoting creativity in our students. As we built on our current understanding of creativity we addressed our misconceptions. Rebecca Hare (2020) led us through a process of what creativity can and should be with her inspiring keynote Practical Creativity: How to Recognize and Cultivate it in Your School. Rebecca led us through a variety of challenges to build our understanding of creativity. She used Torrance's Test for Creative Thinking which is based on five norm referenced measures.

Fluency evaluates the quantity of creative ideas. It is about coming up with several ideas from which to choose. Rebecca explained it can take up to nine ideas before we truly tap into our creativity. Quantity of ideas can indeed lead to quality of ideas.

Originality describes the unusualness of our responses. Do we come up with the expected ideas or do we see new and unanticipated concepts?

Elaboration is how you add your imagination and include details in your work. Can you take something simple and turn it into something entirely different with not only your imagination, but by adding details?

Abstractness of Title is determined by deep, rich thoughts that go beyond the obvious and have us look at things in different ways.

Resistance to Premature Closure asks if we feel drawn to finish things in the easiest way or do we lean in and persevere to find a more innovative way to the finish line.

Before completing these challenges, many would not have entered my mind as being measures of creativity. So many questions flooded my brain. When I think of creativity, was I including all of these? If not, why? Which of these measures was I strongest in and which can I aim to improve as I monitor my own creativity? Was I looking at all of these areas with my students? Where was I limiting creativity? If, as Rebecca expressed, creative thinking was the biggest predictor of lifetime achievement, why wasn't I being inclusive of all measures?

How can technology enhance creativity?

Rebecca explained, "We need to develop *digital literacy* and *creative literacy* in ourselves." As educators, we often use terminology as if we all share the same common understanding of terms. If I have learned anything as I explored the Professional Learning Community (PLC) culture, it is making sure we all have a common understanding of our targets.

Rebecca defined digital literacy as "the ability to find, use, evaluate, and create with a variety of digital tools to express ideas responsibly and ethically." This moved me. So much of what I do as a school-based technology specialist fits in with this idea, not to mention how I use digital resources as I blog.

The idea of creative literacy, however, was new to me. Rebecca says creative literacy is "the ability to create with purpose, use methods and processes to generate new ideas, create with a variety of media, and reflect on and understand creative work." This was a great place to start focusing on myself.

Having identified creative literacy as the area I needed to work on, I challenged myself to incorporate more creative literacy with my learners. One new way I learned to promote creativity was through creative workflow.

Define is the first step of the creative workflow. Students determine their purpose and understand the opportunity before them.

Create happens next. Students brainstorm ideas. They explore, refine and develop the best way to express their ideas. This is where students will find the best media to use for their intended purpose.

Reflect follows. Now, students review their process and their product and discover new insights as they do so.

Reviewing this process, I quickly realized I spend most of my time with students in the *create* section. Some projects also included *define*, while others might touch on *reflect*, but I couldn't easily recall any projects that included all three sections. Could I revise one of my upcoming units to include the creative workflow?

How could I put all this together?

As I began to plan the next sequence of activities for my classes, this seemed to be the perfect time to have students flex their creative muscles.

I decided to try something new. Smithsonian Open Access released three million public domain images for use, remix, and reuse. Since learning about the Smithsonian Learning Lab at Washington International School's Summer Institute for Teachers (WISSIT), I have been impressed by the astounding digital resources available to all of our students. As part of this release, Smithsonian also shared a starter project called "Make a Collagasaurus."

According to Sciezska and Weinberg's companion book, *How to Make a Collagasaurus* (2020), a "collagasaurus" is a collection of public domain images put together to create something new. What a great project to get my students' creative juices flowing.

Employing my own creative workflow, I wanted to define this opportunity for my learners, while still giving my students agency over their own creative workflow. Knowing the students were currently learning about ancient China, I began to explore open resource images. I found about 200 images that would give my students choices while not overwhelming them.

Next, I needed to determine what media my students would use to create their collagasaurus. My students had already used: Google Draw, Wixie, Google Slides, but after my experience the previous weekend, Adobe Spark kept popping into my mind. I decided to use Adobe Spark Post to give my students flexibility in creating while still giving them ease of use.

With my plan defined and in place, it was now time to lead my students through the creative process. I began by reading my students the companion book from the website to spark their curiosity and imagination. Afterwards, we defined their parameters: how many images they should use, how they could refine searches to find what they wanted, and how they would curate the resources they selected.

See it in action:

My students were engaged and very eager to begin their creation experience. We determined ten images was a good place to start and we would store these images in an Ancient China folder in their download folder.

Students were excited as they explored the resources and added them to the designated folder. With their own collections of public domain images downloaded, students started to investigate how to create their "collagasaurus" using the tools in Adobe Spark Post. They clicked and changed the public domain images into something entirely new.

Each time I taught this lesson, I experienced the same sense of wonder. However, it was during the first week of this lesson when something transformative happened.

With about 15 minutes left in the period one student called me over and announced he was done. I tried questing him to see if there was something else he could add, "Nope," he said. I knew he had only just started to access the full breadth of his creativity, so I asked him to remix his images in a new way to find the best possible design. We had explored this idea during the Adobe Creative Educator Day, trying to create multiple ideas before deciding on a final product. The student went back to the drawing board to create another collagasaurus, pushing past his predefined creative limits.

As a technology coach, I have a unique opportunity to infuse creativity into my students' lives. I am not bound by grades, but empowered by standards. A new thought entered my mind. What if my students made multiple collagasauruses, selected one as their final product, then reflected on their creative journey?

Shortly after we began this activity and I started down this creative path, our world changed. Schools closed due to COVID-19 and, in my district, we began emergency remote learning on March 13, 2020. We thought this situation would be temporary, but we learned otherwise. That spring, the focus was on survival and troubleshooting. My skills as a technology coach were put to the test. Our new normal challenged my colleagues and me in ways we could have never imagined. No longer was creativity a focus for me, there was no time.

As we entered virtual teaching, demands on everyone became overwhelming. We were worried about getting almost 900 students connected on their personal devices, followed by troubleshooting all the issues that arose. For quite a while, the last thing I felt was creative. Everything was harder in a COVID world and I had no idea how to connect what I had learned to this new normal.

Inspiring Cognitive Flexibility

During this time, I got the opportunity to participate in the International Society of Technology in Education's (ISTE) Creative Constructor Lab Virtual Conference. After listening to the keynote and participating in my first two sessions, I felt re-energized. I also felt a sense of familiarity. So much of what was shared in this conference echoed the Adobe Creative Educator Day, but also took it a step further. I collected new nuggets of knowledge from these inspiring sessions and for the first time in months, I was filled with creative excitement.

During the keynote, Joseph South, the Chief Learning Officer of ISTE, expressed this thought, "Because they wandered, they were successful." He described how successful people wander, explore, tinker, and how they turn errors into learning experiences. He called this practice cognitive flexibility. As he explained this practice, I made many connections to having a growth mindset.

2020 was truly an exercise in cognitive flexibility. When we think about cognitive flexibility, we consider how we can adapt it to our needs and still move forward.

Indeed, teaching in a virtual environment required all of these skills. It insisted upon dedication to our students and awareness of what they needed. It demanded confidence as we tried new things outside of our comfort zone. We needed to be adaptable, showing flexibility when things did not go as planned. Through all of these struggles, we learned from any missteps we made.

Promoting Creativity in a Remote Learning Environment

Inspiring cognitive flexibility is also important for our students. Allowing them to learn in this way promotes creativity. How we did this in a remote setting was a question I asked myself during the 2020-2021 school year. As a new STEAM teacher, I was very fortunate to be able to collaborate with our school's fabulous STEAM teacher, Mandy Rice. She was phenomenal about sharing her expertise, while welcoming my feedback. We began the year focusing on creativity, having students select an object and present an alternate use for it. Students then explained their object's new use on a Flipgrid. It was so much fun watching them flex their creativity muscles.

During the ISTE Creative Constructor's Lab, I also attended a session by Alicia Johal about robotics and engineering during remote learning. She described how she promotes creativity in her middle school students. Her goal was to provide low entry and high ceiling prototyping challenges with her students. As she implemented her ideas, she promoted projects that were not only empathy-based but centered on helping others. She also discussed how she encouraged the use of digital tools like Google Drawings and Tinkercad in a remote learning environment.

Empowering A Designer's Mindset

The other session I attended during this virtual summit focused on developing a designer's mindset from a distance. Amanda Haughs began her session sharing this quote from David Kelley, "Wallowing in that state of not knowing is not easy, but it's necessary" (2019).

She shared eight design abilities creative problem solvers have and ways she worked with her students to develop these abilities. The diverse focus on these design abilities made me reflect on which skills I had focused on so far during STEAM classes, and which ones I still needed to address. I was also struck by how these design abilities connected with many of my district's Portrait of a Graduate skills.

She shared many ideas for creativity sprints in her presentations. These were simple ideas in which students could use what they had around them to boost creativity. From scavenger hunts to shape drawings and more, these were ideas that could be implemented the next day.

How can you take this expanded view of creativity and bring it to life? Digital tools offer so many ways to amplify student learning. From using scaffolds such as Thinking Routines to create visual representations of student learning to exploring creative processes using these tools, there is something for everyone. We are all creative in so many ways and our creativity is limitless. For more, scan the QR code on the next page.

Post a Techy Note

Share the ways you amplify learning with technology tools using #transform.

Chapter 4
Nurturing and Empowering Student Agency

John Spencer's work (2020) speaks to the continuum for student agency. On the far left is compliance, students complete tasks because they are told to, but have little ownership over the process. In the middle is engagement in which the teacher gets students started but the focus is on involving students in the learning internally. At the far right is empowerment allowing students to take control of their learning. How can we nurture this last type of student agency in our classroom and empower students to be active participants in their learning process? To start we will discuss icon literacy, the language of initiative, and the power of video.

Icon Literacy

What is Icon Literacy?

One day, I was driving to school listening to an episode of Vicki Davis' (2018) 10 Minute Teacher Podcast (@coolcatteacher). Her guest, Pana Asavantana, discussed how she was teaching her kindergarteners the language of computers through icons in the same way she taught them to read by decoding. Pana added these icons to her morning messages and learning thrived. This idea transformed my teaching. I could use this idea to help my kindergarten students. I was struggling with my littlest learners and needed a way to reach them. I contacted Pana via Twitter and she sent me a link to her talk on putting handles on learning.

How to use this to develop student agency:

I began teaching a few icons at a time by embedding them into my greeting message. As my littlest students learned the icons and understood their meaning, their technology proficiency improved. They became more independent and started to use problem solving strategies before asking for help.

I found myself excited about teaching my kindergarteners every week, propelled by their astounding progress. After this success, I began using this strategy with all my students. They became more independent, more able to help themselves when they got stuck.

Another idea percolated in my head as I witnessed their success. Could I reinforce icon literacy for my students in the form of a word wall? My students and I built a phenomenal icon word wall that year. With icons as guides, my students had more agency and became better creators using technology.

The Language of Initiative

What is the Language of Initiative?

During the Washington International School Summer Institute for Teachers (WISSIT), Project Zero ideas Building a Culture of Thinking, Educating for Global Competence, and Maker Thinking in Children, make up the tenets of this unique experience and frame all the learning that occurs each summer.

On the first day Ron Ritchhart, the author of the books *Intellectual Character* (Ritchhart, 2002), *Making Thinking Visible* (Ritchhart, Church, Morrison, 2011) , and *Creating Cultures of Thinking: The 8 Forces We Must Master to Truly Transform Our Schools* (Ritchhart, 2015), hosted a plenary session called Good Talk about Good Teaching. He discussed the eight cultural forces needed to create a culture of thinking and how we can leverage them in our classrooms. He also talked about Project Zero's Our Words Matter and asked, "What do your students hear you say repeatedly?" This made me pause. Were my words promoting a culture of thinking every day?

In the afternoon I chose to attend another one of Ron's sessions called the Importance of Language. It took the morning's plenary session to the next level as he spoke of the language of initiative. I reflected specifically on what messages I conveyed. Did I promote a sense of agency? Did I rescue my students instead of helping them answer their own questions?

This also made me think about the way I responded to both staff and students. In my current position, those responses are so important and set the tone for my interactions with both.

How to use this to develop student agency:
I needed to consider who was doing the thinking. Was I asking questions that promote agency and thinking? Did I convey that I believed the answer was within them?

This metacognitive process continued as I listened to Ron's session the next morning. He discussed Ten Messages in Action for Cultures of Thinking. The third message really resonated with me: to create a new story of learning, we must change the role of student and teacher.

It is said that the person doing the talking is doing all the thinking. Who is talking in our classrooms? Are we supporting our students in becoming active creators, problem solvers, and community members? Are we as teachers focusing on coaching, mentoring, and being community navigators?

To do this requires us to change how we look at teaching. No longer should we be the sage on the stage, but a guide on the side. How can we nurture this process even further, give our students tools to empower them, and use questioning to further drive their ideas and thinking?

The Power of Video

Why use video?

I had the privilege of listening to a keynote given by Catlin Tucker (@Catlin_Tucker) on Concurrent Instruction. One of my big takeaways was the power of asynchronous video. This was shared in a concurrent classroom context, but rings true in any context. Asynchronous video can empower our learners. It allows them to access content at their own pace and provides them with ways to revisit the material as needed.

The power of using asynchronous video became clear to me one afternoon as I introduced the idea of Shapegrams (Vincent, 2019) to my third grade students. Shapegrams, created by Tony Vincent

(@tonyvincent), help students learn how to work in Google Drawings by using and combining shapes. Tony leads these activities by modeling the steps in a video on the Shapegrams website.

The next week, these students would be using Google Drawings to make Google Classroom banners. I wanted to give them a chance to preview this program beforehand and this seemed like a great way to get started.

How to use this to develop student agency:

Although most of my students had never used Google Drawings before, having Tony model the activity really empowered them. Many students revisited the video several times to learn the new skill. Other students would work collaboratively to figure out how to accomplish some of the tasks. After about 30 minutes many asked, "Can we do this at home too?" After working through this lesson with my first class, I was excited to see if all my students would react the same way. When my other classes had the same reaction as the first, I knew I was on to something.

What was it about this activity that worked? The first thing I noticed was how engaged my students were by the video. The combination of music, graphics and hands-on instruction was just right.

The second thing that struck me was how my students continued to be engaged as they worked. They were learning valuable skills as creators of content. These skills would serve the students well as they readied themselves to create Google Classroom banners with Google Drawings.

Icon-Infused Learning

What are Icon-Infused Learning Targets?

After my initial successes with icon literacy and my quest to use the language of initiative in the back of my mind, I diligently set up my icon word wall in the computer lab the next year. I started to consider new ways to up the ante with icon literacy.

How to use this to develop student agency:

Being in a school where we were required to post learning targets, this seemed the next logical place to add icons. I found icons for username and password and many other terms my students needed in the first few sessions.

While this approach worked well with my students, my littlest learners needed something more. They were fidgety and needed movement. Icons alone were not sticky enough for them.

This led me to make signs for important words. Using principles of Whole Brain Teaching, students learned signs for username, password, and more. Username was seven fingers, since their usernames were seven digits. Password was a lock because it was our secret words and numbers.

After teaching these signs, I linked them to icons. This made the process more concrete for my kindergarteners and worked better than using a typical morning message greeting. However, as the year continued, the way I shared directions with students needed to change.

These directions started to become more of an algorithm or a list of steps for my students. Using a visual list of steps set up an environment engineered for success. Every student could access the content using the icon literacy skills we had developed. Students did not always need to ask me for help. They could help themselves by looking at the board first.

Empowering Student Agency Using Student Voice

What opportunities do you provide for your students to express their voices? Are you communicating that their voices matter? How do you create learning experiences to empower learners? These are all key questions we should consider as we plan engaging experiences for students. As George Couros and Katie Novak explain in *Innovate Inside the Box: Empowering Learners Through UDL and the Innovator's Mindset* (2019), "Empowering is about ownership and agency. Providing opportunities for voice and choice in learning experiences is how we create learning experiences that empower learners."

Empowering student voice is more than just educational buzz. Nationwide, states have adopted Future Ready Skills, sometimes known as the 5 Cs: Critical Thinking, Creative Thinking, Communication, Collaboration, Citizenship. Empowering student voice allows students to both develop and demonstrate these skills by sharing their ideas and explaining why their ideas are good. As they create a plan to share their thinking and their new learning, they build vital communication skills. When they use their voices to try new things and take risks to show their creative side, they flex their creative thinking skills. In addition, they grow their collaboration skills by seeing things from other people's points of view. They build citizenship skills, and become part of a caring and responsible digital community.

How can we best do this? What are some ways we can give students opportunities for both voice and choice? In my work as a technology specialist, I have discovered some technology tools that are especially well suited to honor both voice and choice.

#1 Wixie

Why use this tool to empower student voice:

Wixie has a simple interface that is easy for younger students to use their voice, video, and royalty free clip art to share their ideas. It also allows collaboration with Wixie Teams tools. In addition to the easy to use student interface, the teacher dashboard is comprehensive and makes it easy to review, comment on, and manage student work.

How to use this tool to empower student voice:

My first graders used Wixie to share their understanding of a force's impact on an object. Students first read an article about forces on Pebble Go, a kid friendly database. Then, each student created a picture of a force acting on an object. At this point, students had a choice of either adding voice or video to explain their creation. These were compiled into class books so the students could see each others' final projects.

Another of my classes used this program to create Digital Citizenship Pledges based on how they would share, respond, work or play online. This time they used the audio and video options to demonstrate their critical thinking skills and explain why their idea was a good one.

#2 Flipgrid's Shorts Camera

Why use this tool to empower student voice:

When Flipgrid released the Shorts Camera, students could customize their videos at a higher level. Features like whiteboard, blackboard and the ability to create multiple segments as part of one video gave Flipgrid superpowers. Students can show their thinking as they solve math problems or practice reciting several pieces of poetry without being on camera.

How to use this tool to empower student voice:

One of my classes used the Shorts camera to demonstrate how they solved a task called Packing for Algebraland. Students needed to determine how much more they could include in their packed luggage and explain why. Several students took advantage of these camera features when creating their responses.

Another class presented and recited poetry. Reciting poetry can be overwhelming, but using Flipgrid's features helped not only build their confidence, but demonstrate their voice.

#3 Pear Deck

Why use this tool to empower student voice:

Pear Deck's interactive platform allows all students to be active participants in class and express their voice. Whether in a virtual,

73

hybrid, or face to face classroom, it is a game changer. Students engage in the lessons and work is shared and discussed anonymously, giving shy students a level of ease.

How to use this tool to empower student voice:

Pear Deck is a great resource to use for math. In one of my classes we used this to look at different ways to solve unit rate problems. One of the problems they needed to solve was: *Kallie ran ⅕ mile in 1 ½ minutes. At this rate, how long would it take her to run 1 mile?*

Every student had a different approach to solving this problem. For example, one student multiplied ½ x 5 and then 1 x 5 and added the products together. Another student drew a number line divided into fifths and then labeled each length in 1 ½ intervals to get the same answer. Both got the correct answer, but used different ways to solve it. Exposing our students to other ways of thinking is vital.

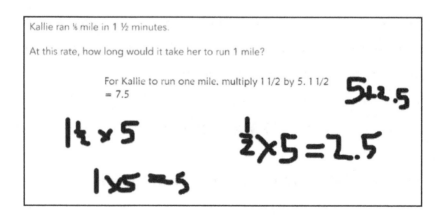

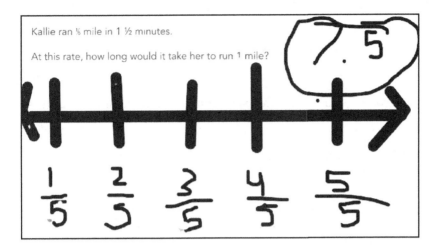

Kallie ran ⅕ mile in 1 ½ minutes.

At this rate, how long would it take her to run 1 mile?

7.5

$\frac{1}{5}$ $\frac{2}{5}$ $\frac{3}{5}$ $\frac{4}{5}$ $\frac{5}{5}$

Pear Deck also works when reflecting on favorite activities. Some of my students used it to share their favorite activity during distance learning. Since they put their reflections on a drawing slide, they had the option of using text, drawing, or a combination of both.

These examples exhibit just a few ways we can use technology tools to empower student voice. This is by no means an all inclusive list, just some favorite tools that help me as an educator. This list is always growing and I am excited to see what I can add to my toolbox next.

Creating with Storytelling

In Zaretta Hammond's book, *Culturally Responsive Teaching and the Brain: Promoting Authentic Engagement and Rigor Among Culturally and Linguistically Diverse Students* (2014), she explained, "The brain is wired to remember stories and to use the story structure to make sense of the world. That's why every culture has creation stories. In oral traditions, stories play a bigger role in teaching lessons about manners, morality, or simply what plants to eat or not eat in the wilderness because it's the way content is remembered. Diverse students (and all students, really) learn content more effectively if they can create a coherent narrative about the topic or process presented. That's the brain's way of weaving it all together. (Bonus: It also offers a great way to check for understanding and correct misconceptions.)"

When we amplify learning, we make it sticky and storytelling is a powerful way to accomplish this. Digital storytelling usually consists of a combination of computer based images, text, audio, video and music. Below are some ways technology helps us to share our voices and stories.

#1 Podcasting

Why use this product to empower student voice:
Podcasts are very popular in today's society. The idea of an audio recording you can listen to anywhere, anytime has exploded. Podcasting tools have gotten much easier to use and are now accessible to all of our students allowing them to tell their stories.

Many programs can be used to help students create podcasts. I prefer to have students use tools with which they are already familiar, are easy to use, and can be taken to go if needed.

Some options to get started:

Wixie is so easy to use. Each page could consist of a podcast episode that can be saved and edited in multiple sessions. Files saved as an mp4 can be easily turned into an audio file. There is also a massive library of stickers and pictures to use for episode artwork.

Flipgrid is also easy to use, but unlike Wixie, it is free and does not require a subscription. Students can use the microphone only option to create a sound file without any video or they can use the stickers and pictures to create episode artwork. To use Flipgrid, the teacher would need to start a topic or grid for students to use and all work would need to happen in one session.

#2 Comic Strips

Why use this product to empower student voice:

"Comics and cartoons are a great way to engage students in the stories they are reading, the information they are researching, and the ideas they are exploring in your curriculum." (Wixie, 2021) In recent years, graphic novels and comic books have become increasingly popular. Why not have students use this format to tell stories? So many of our students are artistic and this is a great way to empower them.

Some options to get started:

Like podcasting, many programs can be used to make comics online. The two I recommend, Wixie and Google Slides, are extremely similar. They both require student logins, have multiple pages and can be used collaboratively over multiple sessions. Essentially, they each allow you to use their slideshow format to create frames for your comic strips.

The biggest differences between the two are in their ease of use and cost. Wixie is easier to use and has a large library of stickers and pictures that are public domain and royalty free, but Wixie requires a subscription. Google Slides is free. While using Google Slides, students need to be mindful of what copyright restrictions exist on any pictures they use.

#3 eBooks

Why use this product to empower student voice:

Everyone likes to see published student work. Parents and students alike enjoy sharing student creations and eBooks give that option in a very unique way. The team at Creative Educator honestly says this best, "Creating ePubs, or digital books, makes it easy to share and distribute student work. While students love a book they can touch, creating print versions of student work can be cost-prohibitive. eBooks can be shared online and easily distributed to families and friends in faraway places. They can be read and enjoyed on smartphones by parents at work and students in school." (Creative Educator, 2014)

Some options to get started:

Students in classrooms today use eBooks all the time to access digital information. Why not give our students the opportunity to publish and share their own digital books? As with the comic books, both Wixie and Google Slides continue to be good options. Wixie even allows you to export your work in an epub file. Another program to consider is Adobe Spark Video. It has many of the same features of the programs mentioned before and is simple to use. If you can click it, you can change it.

Empowering Student Agency with HyperDocs

One of the best ways we can empower our students is with voice and choice. We want them to be more self directed learners. This doesn't happen immediately and needs to be scaffolded along the way. Two great ways to do this are using HyperDocs and Choice Boards.

Created by Lisa Highfill, Kelly Hilton and Sarah Landis (2016), HyperDocs make a digital framework to deliver lesson content focusing on collaboration, communication, creativity, and critical thinking. The content is packaged in one digital tool, often Google Slides or Docs. There are a variety of different templates available for HyperDocs and all focus on students reflecting and synthesizing their knowledge.

Ocean PBL Project

What were students working on?

At one point my students were studying oceans. Each of the science units in my district has a Project Based Learning component and we decided to use a HyperDoc as a means of delivering this content. We chose the model: Engage, Explore and Apply.

During Engage, students used EdPuzzle to watch two videos centering on the impact of plastic on the complex systems of the oceans. After watching these videos independently, students worked collaboratively to create a headline for the content on Padlet. This got students involved and ready to learn.

In Explore, students began their research. We set up a collaborative Slide Deck to help each group organize their notes and inside the HyperDocs were all the resources needed.

For Apply, students worked together to create a Google site to share what they had learned. Each site needed to include some type of video, an original graphic and needed to answer the three overarching questions of the project.

How did this empower student agency?

Using this format, not only empowered students but gave them access to everything they needed. During the Explain portion of the project, students could choose which of the many resources they wanted to use for their research. In the Apply section, students could choose from several different options to create their videos and images.

Empowering Student Agency with Choice Boards

If you have ever listened to Kasey Bell (@ShakeUpLearning) you know how much she appreciates Choice Boards. When I read her new book, *Shake Up Learning: Practice Ideas to Move from Static to Dynamic* (Bell, 2018), I was immediately enamored with this idea of incorporating both choice and voice into my assignments using Choice Boards.

One of the Choice Boards Kasey talks about is a Tic Tac Toe Choice Board. All students must complete square #5 in the center of the board. Then, they get a choice of two other boxes they can complete to get a tic tac toe. As a school-based technology specialist, I work with students in technology classes on a weekly basis. I often used strategies such as the Tic Tac Toe Board to provide students choices on how they demonstrate their knowledge. I also use this to model digital differentiation for staff and students. Here are a few examples of how I have used Choice Boards over the years.

Example of Tic Tac Toe Board

1 — Use **Flipgrid** to share your answers to your 3 research questions.	2 — Use **Chatterpix** to share your answers to your 3 research questions.	3 — Use the **Wixie** trading card template to share your answers to your 3 research questions.
4 — Use **Puppet Pals** to share your answers to your 3 research questions.	5 — **Review Design Your Own Monument** and then answer your 3 research questions for your blue boxes:	6 — **Create a Monument: Minecraft style** Use Tinkercad to create a model for your famous American using the Minecraft style.
7 — **Create a Monument: Lego style** Use **Tinkercad** to create a model for your famous American using the Minecraft style.	8 — **Create a Monument: Basic Tinkercad** Use **Tinkercad** to create a model for your famous American using the Minecraft style.	9 — **Create a Monument: Basic Tinkercad** Use **Tinkercad** to create a model for your famous American using the Minecraft style.

What were students working on?

Famous Americans Tic Tac Toe Board

My grade level team brought a project to me in which students were to research a famous American then create a monument using Tinkercad to convey information about that individual. At first, I was not quite sure how to proceed as I had never used Tinkercad. Moreover, I wanted to make this project my own. The previous school-based technology specialist at my school was kind enough to walk me through Tinkercad, so my first problem was solved.

Next problem, how to make this project my own. As I looked at the questions, Flipgrid popped into my mind, but were there other ways to incorporate choice and voice for boxes 6-9? I went to the digital ecosystem library and found a few more options. Then I realized this was becoming a Tic Tac Toe Choice Board.

Boxes 1-4 focused on tools to share the answers to three questions. What makes our famous American so important? Why did you choose your famous American? What message do you want people to think of when they see your monument?

I chose two options the students were familiar with: Flipgrid and Wixie. I also chose two iPad options: ChatterPix and Puppet Pals. For boxes 6-9 I wanted students to build their 3D monuments in Tinkercad using Minecraft and Lego options.

I was all ready to start, but I had never used a Choice Board with students in this grade level. How could I explain it to them?

First we discussed why we called this a Tic Tac Toe Board. Then I explained that everyone *must* complete the white #5 box in the center and how to get Tic Tac Toe.

Starting in box #5, students built their background knowledge about monuments using an electronic book linked to the menu square. They read all about the Washington Monument and the World War II memorial. They also read ideas about designing monuments and watched a video for ideas.

How did this empower student agency?

After that, I explained each of the tools in boxes 1-4 the students could choose from to complete their project: Flipgrid, Chatterpix, Wixie, or Puppet Pals..

Boxes 6-9 provided students with choices on how they used Tinkercad. Tinkercad has three different design modes. Students could use the traditional 3D models, blocks (what they refer to as Minecraft mode) or bricks (Lego mode).

Finally, I laid out a set of instructions for them to scaffold the activity into easy to follow steps.

Ancient Egypt Tic Tac Toe Choice Boards

Students were asked to research an invention or contribution to modern society from ancient Egypt, then report what they learned. I was excited to create a Tic Tac Toe Choice Board for this project.

To begin, students used Padlet to look at a map of Egypt and state a See, Think, Wonder. Then, they watched a video or read/listened to a book about an invention or contribution from ancient Egypt. After that, they shared three things they learned using Flipgrid.

I found two pages on each invention from an online resource and asked students to complete a 3-2-1 organizer for their chosen invention. I knew the students working on the Egypt project would need some scaffolding for this format, so I again used a student algorithm with icons to build their understanding.

How did this empower student agency?
This process allowed students to learn about ancient Egypt in multiple ways. Then, students displayed what they learned on the collaborative platform of Flipgrid in a simple one-page format that could be combined into a collaborative book.

The students in our classrooms today are the future leaders of tomorrow. We need to not only nurture them to promote student agency, but empower them. From our youngest to our oldest learners, we can do this in many ways. The technology tools are available, we just need to reach out and use them. Want to extend your learning? Scan the QR code on the next page.

Post a Techy Note

Share how you are harnessing technology to nurture and empower student agency using #transform.

Chapter 5

Seeking Connections Beyond Your School

I've heard it said frequently if you're not a connected educator you are missing out. No educator needs to be on an island in today's world. If you are initially resistant, I completely understand. I only joined Twitter in 2017 and did so reluctantly .

Using Twitter to Tell My Classroom's Story

My principal, while working in Fairfax County Public Schools, was an avid Twitter user. She was a connected educator and wanted to empower her staff to use social media to promote all the great things happening at our school.

When I first joined Twitter I was skeptical, to say the least. I thought Twitter was a platform for outspoken politicians and celebrities. It had taken me a long time to even try Facebook and now I would be tweeting? I reluctantly created a Twitter handle, @MrsTannenb, and shared it and my school's hashtag, #FHESFamily, with my students' families.

I quickly found Twitter to be a more meaningful way to tell my class' and school's story. As my team and I implemented fresh ideas such as PBL and Portrait of a Graduate skills (21st Century Skills), I learned how to hashtag my posts with #FCPSPOG and #PBLinFCPS.

Using Twitter to Learn (Incognito)

My Twitter Incognito use started slowly. I first saw a post my principal had retweeted so I "liked" that post. Then, I decided to follow the person who originally posted the tweet. As I followed more people, I found wonderful content in their posts.

Before I knew it, I was spending time scrolling through my feed to learn. With so many intelligent educators on Twitter, there is a wealth of knowledge to gain. When I started out on Twitter, I was consumed with all the content. It was energizing to see all the innovative ideas in my feed.

Seeking Other Connections via Podcasts

A while ago, I attended a workshop on Executive Functioning. Although the content of the workshop was extremely valuable, it was a connection I made that had the biggest impact. Another member of the workshop mentioned he had started listening to a podcast called ADHD Essentials (Mahan, 2018) and how helpful it was in working with his students. I started listening to it right away, having two step-children and a husband with attention deficit hyperactivity disorder (ADHD), I was eager to learn more.

I wondered what other podcasts were out there that could forward my education. During a random search, I found Google Teacher Tribe. This podcast started my educational technology podcast obsession. Immediately I found myself waiting for Monday morning so I could listen to Matt and Kasey. They had such a dynamic rapport. I couldn't believe how much I learned just by listening to a podcast on my way to work. I started following the Google Teacher Tribe podcast as well as Kasey Bell and Matt Miller on Twitter.

When Kasey stated that her book, *Shake Up Learning: Practical Ideas to Move Learning from Static to Dynamic* (2018) was being released, I knew I had to read it. Just like Google Teacher Tribe, her book spoke to me. It quickly became my go-to when it came to educational technology.

After discovering the Google Teacher Tribe podcast, I began to find other educational technology podcasts, including Kasey's Shake Up Learning. We live in a time where not only are so many connected educators sharing their voices, but they have created communities for their listeners as well. Now, my commute to work is peppered with educational podcasts, each one offering unique insights.

Adjacent Possible Moments

The podcast Educational Duct Tape by Jake Miller (@JakeMillerTech) focuses on how we can use technology to solve problems or meet an educational need. This quickly became my hump-day podcast, giving me a boost of energy every Wednesday.

Each week, he discusses what he calls a "soapbox moment." During one of these moments, he shared the theory of adjacent possible moments, "Adjacent possible moments happen when a new set of possibilities is enabled by taking one step beyond the current state of things. Every step opens up new possibilities, just like every conversation with a person can lead to new possibilities that you had not considered." So many adjacent possible moments have occurred for me as I connected to others outside of my school through podcasts. These moments have transformed my life and career.

#CSinSF and How an Adjacent Possible Moment Led to New Connections

I was listening to #EduDuctTape by Jake Miller on the way to school one morning. Jake was interviewing Karly Moura (@KarlyMoura) and discussing ways to enhance communication and add to your computer science curriculum. They mentioned Computer Science in San Francisco (#CSinSF), a computer science curriculum for kindergarten through eighth grade students based in San Francisco that is accessible to anyone.

When I explored #CSinSF, I was so impressed I decided to tweet out a thanks to Jake Miller, Karly Moura, and #CSinSF. I could have never imagined what would happen as a result. Firstl, Jake Miller responded to my post. Even more exciting, Karly Moura was now following me! Plus, Bill Marsland (@billmarsland), who works at #CSinSF wanted my feedback on his curriculum. WOW!

#CSinSF will be one of your adjacent possible moments. This interaction would have never happened without Twitter. It has allowed me to learn so many new things and has linked me to educators around the world.

Getting Google Certified Because of Podcasts

Being a faithful listener to the Google Teacher Tribe for close to a year, I was using G Suite (now called Google Workspace) regularly in my classroom. On her podcast, Kasey Bell regularly shared how impactful it was to get her Google Certifications. She frequently referred to it as life changing.

I decided to kick things up a notch and take the Level I Google Certified Educator exam. This exam was no joke. It was a three hour exam and I used close to all my time. I was so excited to have passed! This certification validated for both myself and my school community that I possessed basic competencies using G Suite for Education. It also affirmed that I was dedicated to using this tool with both my staff and students to create transformative educational experiences. Ready for the next challenge, I took the Level 2 Google Certified Educator (GCE) exam. Once again, I sat down for another three hour exam and used close to all my time, making sure I showed how much I knew about Google. Like last time, I was thrilled to pass the exam!

Twitter Chats. What's That?

In my original technology coach position, one of the first breakfast training sessions I held was "Tweet and Eat." I wanted to share Twitter early because I felt this technology tool was a game changer. At that time, I had been using Twitter for over a year. As I compiled training materials, I remember wondering how to include information on Twitter chats, never having tried one myself.

I decided to try a local one, #NoVAEdChat, to get my feet wet. This Northern Virginia Educational Chat is held Wednesday nights and moderated by technology coaches. Every day, there are Twitter chats happening. They vary in subject and focus, but are great ways to connect outside of your school. Some of my favorites are #TeachBetter, #leadlap, and #pd4uandme. Search Education Chats on Twitter and find one that interests you.

Most Twitter chats follow a set format where a certain number of questions are asked and participants respond with the number of questions asked. For Question 1 (Q1), your answer will be A1. During the chat, not only do you get the opportunity to answer the questions yourself, but also see others' responses and comment on them. By participating you are sure to find beneficial connections outside of your school.

Regarding those connections, conduct a social media audit. Make sure you are getting a variety of perspectives that represent different positions, cultures, etc. One big reason for seeking connections is to expand your horizons as you encounter new perspectives and consider them in your educational practice.

Making Connections Around the Country and Beyond

All of these experiences made me want to gain more knowledge and more connections. Another great way to seek connections beyond your school is to attend conferences.

In *Innovate Inside The Box: Empowering Learning Through UDL and the Innovator's Mindset* (Couros and Novak, 2019), George Couros says, "To be a master educator, you must also be a master learner." He asserts, "In a profession where learning is the focus of our job, growth is essential and the target is always moving."

He is not alone in this mindset. In *The Four O'clock Faculty: A Rogue Guide to Revolutionizing Professional Development* (Czyz, 2017), Rich Czyz states, "Whatever you are and whatever you do, whether you are an administrator or teacher or instructional coach, remember that the best thing you can do to improve learning for your students is to improve learning for yourself."

As educators, we need to be models of lifelong learning and the common pursuit of learning is a great way to make connections. So when I got the opportunity to attend the ISTE conference in Philadelphia, I took it. I was totally out of my comfort zone. It had been a long time since I had traveled on my own, but my desire to have this experience was greater than my fear.

One of the highlights of the ISTE conference was, again, making great connections. From the moment I entered the Pennsylvania Convention Center, connections were a huge part of this conference experience. I met a great many people and everyone was very approachable. Afterall, we are all educators here to determine how technology could help our students reach their learning goals.

I was fangirling hard when I met some of my eduheroes like Matt Miller (@jmattmiller), Jake Miller (@JakeMillerTech), Kasey Bell (@shakeuplearning), Karly Moura (@karlymoura), Eric Curts (@ericcurts), Chris Nesi (@mrnesi). It meant a lot to me to be able to thank the educators I followed on social media. As time went by, rather than fangirling, I was just connecting with other educators who were part of my tribe.

Getting to meet other educators in real life who I have followed and corresponded with was fabulous. Making in person connections with my virtual PLN made the connections more concrete and added a new dimension to many of those prior connections. Meeting people from around the world and continuing to build my PLN was a marvelous experience.

Consider an EdCamp

Conferences like ISTE can be expensive. If you are fortunate, your school may assist you with funding. For those of us who don't have this luxury, there are many low cost or no cost conferences available to help educators learn and build connections.

For the first 45 minutes at EdCamp NoVa, people talk and add ideas for sessions to the schedule. They enjoy breakfast as the day is planned, then everyone is called together. The sessions had been determined and announced. At EdCamp, you can select the sessions you want to attend and if they aren't meeting your needs, you can feel free to choose another session.

The variety of sessions at an EdCamp is extensive. At the one I attend, there are no leaders. Conversations happen organically and communal notes are taken for each session on a Google Doc linked to the EdCamp schedule. Everyone is there to learn and each room has a different topic. One of the best things about an EdCamp is the cost. It is FREE! You cannot get better than that for a Saturday morning of professional development.

I find going to events like these makes me push myself by being exposed to new perspectives. Building connections and experiencing the contagious excitement of passionate educators who are committed to their students is gratifying.

You do not need to be confined to the walls of your school to make connections. There are so many wonderful opportunities, take a risk and push yourself. Seeking connections beyond school benefits you, and ultimately your students, with new ideas, collaboration, and innovation.

Try something new to build those connections. Join Twitter, if you haven't. Find an EdCamp. Listen to a podcast. Any of these are great ways to connect. Just open the door, there is an exciting new world waiting for you.

Post a Techy Note

Share how you are seeking connections beyond your school using #transform

Chapter 6
Finding your PLN

As I shared in chapter one, becoming a connected educator changed my life in many ways. One monumental change was building my professional learning network (PLN). Before joining Twitter, I couldn't possibly imagine having lasting and personal relationships with people I met online. Initially, I thought Twitter was just for politicians and celebrities, but I was wrong. Twitter has transformed many educators' lives for many reasons.

Sometimes when you want to try new things you are met with resistance at your school. As the only technology coach in my building, it can feel isolating. We need collaboration to thrive as lifelong learners.

Finding your PLN can be a gradual process. The first thing you need to do is to get connected. There are many types of social media to do this, but for me, it all started by using Twitter.

Getting Started using Twitter

When I started using Twitter, it was relatively new to my school. My principal, Jen Hertzberg (@tchrwithatitle), was on Twitter and quickly made sure our school had a hashtag, #FHESFamily. Then, she encouraged staff members to join. Many of us hesitantly jumped on the bandwagon and shared our Twitter handles with our students and their families.

My principal praised our risk-taking. She created a bulletin board at the entrance of our school, posting all the staff who had started Twitter accounts. I started off by following those teachers. They became part of my PLN as I viewed their posts and gained insights into their classrooms. I would stop by the other classrooms and tell the teachers I had enjoyed their posts. These visits built a community. Sometimes, I would veer off my usual path to visit other classrooms when I saw on my Twitter feed they were doing innovative things. We have so much talent in our own schools, but until we share it, these talents may remain hidden.

After that, I started noticing that many departments in my district had Twitter handles and hashtags associated with them. I followed those departments and expanded my PLN. I read about colleagues doing amazing things when they tagged departments and added hashtags to their posts. I also searched hashtags to see if I could connect with other colleagues with similar interests. For example, searching #edtech helped me connect with other educational technology teachers.

Next, I started following programs I was using with my students. Programs like Flipgrid and PearDeck have huge social media presences. Looking through their feed is a great way to make connections. Other programs like Padlet, EdPuzzle and Google for Education are also great places to get started. Many of these programs also have hashtags. If you look up #flipgridfever or #flipgridforall, you will find great ideas and fantastic educators you can connect to your PLN.

As the year progressed, I began following authors and people from podcasts who inspired me. Inexplicably I felt a connection to these people I had never met face to face. I remember when I bought *Shake Up Learning* (2018) by Kasey Bell and tagged her in a tweet she responded. I felt special, like a connection had been made that would have never been possible without Twitter.

By the end of the school year, I couldn't imagine not having a Twitter account. In one year, my entire experience as an educator had changed. I went from being part of a school, to part of a worldwide network of educators. Not only did I learn a tremendous amount, but I had built connections with many other educators.

Learning from these educators and sharing my classroom gave me a confidence I previously lacked, which transformed me. I even applied to be a school based technology specialist in my district and got a position at a nearby school.

Being part of a group like the School Based Technology Specialists(SBTS), also helped me build my PLN. Using the #fcpsSBTS, I was able to easily share what I was doing. Plus I was able to see what other school based technology specialists in my district were doing and connect with them. It created a community feel in a job where sometimes you can feel like you are on an island in your building. In today's world of social media, no one should feel alone in their classroom.

Tweet and Eat

The first training I hosted as a technology specialist was a "Tweet and Eat." It was the most popular event I held that year. People gathered together on an October morning to learn about the benefits of a PLN. I invited some of the teachers, who were already using Twitter, to explain why they did so.

"Twitter has been a powerful communication tool for me as a school counselor, enabling me to share information about my role and the life skills students gain from our work on academic, personal/social and career domains," Sharon Powers (@CounselorPowers)

"Having a classroom Twitter has served as a wonderful tool to keep parents up to date with what the students are learning in the classroom. I think the parents enjoy being able to see their kids actively participating in the classroom," Brittany Cardenas (@MsCardenasVES)

"I like the ability to share what we are doing in class with parents and coworkers. Parents have mentioned enjoying seeing pictures of their kiddos engaging in classwork," Brittany Long (@MrsLongVES)

It was a phenomenal experience that not only helped my school better tell its story, but connect my colleagues with their own PLNs. A special education teacher told me how she loved seeing what was going on in other rooms of our school. Being connected on Twitter helped teachers build community inside the walls of our school and enhance our school culture. One day, a teacher ran into the staff lounge and said that she felt like a dork, but was so excited. She had tagged someone she was following in a tweet and he responded to her!! I told her I understood, no need to feel like a dork, I had been there and felt that, too. And it's awesome!!

Next Steps Building a PLN

I began to explore other types of social media to see what benefits they might hold. Many podcasts had formed communities using hashtags and they began migrating to Facebook as private groups. Other communities formed private chats on Twitter. These private groups are one of my go-tos as an education technology specialist.

Shake Up Learning

Shake Up Learning is an outstanding community on Facebook created by Kasey Bell. This dynamic community gives educators a place to connect, ask questions, and share their experiences about the Shake Up Learning process.

Kasey also started a podcast called the Shake Up Learning Show that gives helpful tips and has informative interviews. Kasey posts a weekly question and encourages educators to connect and share with her using all forms of social media.

Educational Duct Tapers

Jake Miller hosts a podcast called Educational Duct Tape. I had been following Jake on Twitter and decided to check this out. I was quickly hooked. I appreciated his zany personality and the way he used educational technology as a solution to a problem. Each Wednesday a new guest taught listeners something new. I found myself following Jake's guests on Twitter and making them part of my PLN. Many listeners, myself included, began referring to themselves as "duct tapers" and joined Jake's Educational Duct Tapers community on Facebook.

Teachers on Fire

Tim Cavey, of the Teachers on Fire podcast, profiles leaders from the educational community every week. Each episode starts with a moment of adversity, acknowledging the role failure can have in growth. After listening to his interviews I come away brimming with ideas. These leaders will inspire you and would be great additions to your PLN. Tim also created a Facebook group where educators can celebrate their successes and get support for their non-successes. It is a marvelous community of support and learning.

THRIVEinEDU

THRIVEinEDU is a Facebook community created in response to the struggles of the 2020-2021 school year. Rachelle Dene Poth created this community to connect educators so they could support each other during one of the most difficult years in education.

#pd4uandme Bloggers

A while back I discovered the #pd4uandme chat. This is a 30 minute chat on Saturday mornings that uses an edcamp style format. During a chat I was invited to join their #pd4uandme blogging group, which is a group message chat on Twitter. Becoming part of a group with a common interest gave me some wonderful bloggers to connect with online. It also helped provide me with accountability as I got ready to blog each week.

Teach Better Team and Becoming an Ambassador

The Teach Better Team is another great place to find and connect with other educators. Their motto is to teach better tomorrow than today. The team is a powerhouse of connections. They have an online academy that covers educational topics and instructional strategies, including their signature Grid Method. In addition, they have a very active Facebook group, along with Twitter and Instagram accounts. They also host a podcast that airs at least twice a week.

I began my involvement with the Teach Better Team by participating in Teach Better's #TeachBetter chat on Thursday nights. Then I started listening to the Teach Better podcast. I thoroughly enjoy both, so when I heard they would be online for 12 hours straight, I had to participate.

The Teach Better Team 12 hour live stream event had giveaways and great conversations. During this live stream they announced the start of the Teach Better Ambassador program. They explained that a Teach Better Ambassador was a dedicated educator who embodies the Teach Better mindset. They wanted their ambassadors to share this mindset with others.

They were only taking 25 new members. I was delighted to be chosen in this inaugural group of founding ambassadors. This group has been a beneficial addition to my PLN. We meet monthly and belong to a private Facebook group. Finding a group of like minded educators to connect with is a great way to expand your PLN.

Becoming a Regional Pear Deck Coach

I was so happy when I completed my regional Pear Deck coach training. I was proud to add this certification to my technology toolbox. This company listens to teacher and student feedback and works tirelessly to make learning interactive and give students a voice in their learning. This is demonstrated by Pear Deck's recent additions of Immersive Reader capabilities and the ability to add audio.

I am proud to share my love of Pear Deck with other educators and let them see how, in difficult and unprecedented times like these, this tool can connect our students and give them a chance to share their voices during both synchronous and asynchronous instruction.

I am so grateful to Michelle Meshover, a fellow technology coach and regional Pear Deck coach, for inviting me to a Pear Deck session last summer. This is where I met Robert Yoo, Pear Deck employee and wonderful resource. A special thank you as well to Risa Bennett, for her support leading our virtual cohort through training.

Regional Coaches for Pear Deck connect through a back channel called Slack. We share ideas and give feedback about Pear Deck. I am grateful to be part of a worldwide network that supports a product I believe in.

I have spent most of this chapter giving Twitter and Facebook groups accolades. I believe these are the best places to get started because that is what worked for me. Other places to look for connections include Instagram, LinkedIn, Clubhouse, Voxer and YouTube.

Social media continues to grow and develop. In many ways it's like being in a candy store. Trying to take it all in can be quite overwhelming. Add to your PLN at your own pace. If you haven't added me yet, please follow @TannenbaumTech. I can't wait to learn with you along our collaborative journey.

Post a Techy Note

Share as you build your PLN using #transform.

Chapter 7

Offering Your Voice and Sharing Your Journey!

Establishing a PLN gives you connections through which you can grow. In the beginning you might post some content, but if you are like me, that content is mostly tweets with photographs. Like everyone else, you too have a story to tell and you can do so by adding your voice to more conversations. Taking that leap from being a consumer of content to a creator of content can be scary, but starting with small manageable steps helps a lot!

Consuming Content

When you attend a large conference you can sometimes get lost in hashtags. It would be very easy to go back to your hotel room at the end of the day and scroll your Twitter feed. This is not altogether a bad thing. Using Twitter to find out about other things happening at the conference and building your PLN is good. During my conference experience I found the benefits of being part of my Twitter feed.

It is interesting to me how many of the people I meet at conferences describe themselves as introverts or shy. I certainly felt that way, but getting out of your comfort zone helps you grow and empathize with your students and other teachers when they need to try new things. Sometimes you need to take a chance and be part of the action. Going to smaller events, like CoffeeEdu, allows you to have a more informal experience. Attending any event where everyone has similar interests is a great way to build your PLN.

Creating Content

Attending these events is a great first step, but if you participate, you can amplify the impact by tweeting out about it. Events such as #FlipgridLIVE gives you access to helpful app updates and more. Participating in these types of events links you to your community in a different way. For example, during #FlipgridLIVE, many great updates were unveiled. I posted my reflections and reactions with each new update building personalized connections to vendors.

Starting a Blog

I decided to join two Twitter book studies. In #isteten and #edumagic we read *Edumagic* (Fecich, 2018) and in #ETCoaches we read *Learning Supercharged* (Summerfield and Schrum, 2018). On Day two of both of these book studies, participants were asked to share their website or blog to help others get to know them. I had neither of the two at that time, but enthusiastically shared my Twitter feed. As I read both of these books, the idea of reflection was a common theme. Both texts explained how important reflection was as a learner and an educator.

So I took a risk and created my website, Techy Notes. I was nervous about it so, before I shared it with the world, I sent a link to Sam Fecich (@SFecich), the moderator of the #EduMagic Twitter book study. Her feedback was invaluable. She loved my blog and website and wanted me to share my story. Bravely, I clicked Publish and sent my voice out into the world.

There are many programs available to publish a blog, WordPress and Wix, among others. I decided to use Google Sites. This was a platform I was familiar with, which made clicking Publish seem less scary. I looked at other websites and decided to keep my navigation simple: Home, About Me, Blog, and Social Media. You can post a blog but until someone knows about it, it remains private. Initially, I just shared posts on Twitter. Now I also post on Facebook, Medium, and LinkedIn.

Why a Blog?

This experience alone did not lead me to writing a blog. I read *Be REAL: Educate from the Heart* (2018) by Tara Martin. In this book, she shares her REAL framework:

Relatable

Expose Vulnerability

Approachable

Learn Through Life

In the Learn Through Life section, a key point is how your website can document your journey. It can act as a personal history book that allows you to share your REAL self with the world. Remember, everyone has a story. Don't be afraid to share it. When I first sent my blog and website to Sam Fecich, she wrote back, "Get it out of draft mode and put it out there for the world. More people need to hear your story. It is one of changing positions, supporting teachers and your excitement for edtech which is oozing off every page. I love it!"

These words meant so much to me and propelled me forward. So many times, we are afraid to click the Publish button and don't take that leap. Posting a blog requires vulnerability and open reflection which can seem like a risk, but the rewards are worth it.

Blog for yourself first, but you never know who will be inspired by it. When I look at how many posts I have published , it astounds me.

Going through the blogging process helped me, but others have shared how they were inspired by it as well. To all of you who have shared, thank you so very much.

As you blog, you model digital leadership. In *Social LEADia: Moving Students from Digital Citizenship to Digital Leadership* (2017) Jennifer Casa-Todd notes how important it is that we acknowledge blogging, texting, and tweeting on social media as real writing. Educators need to model these platforms and show students authentic uses for writing. By doing this, we encourage our students to also engage in these mediums. Jennifer claims that digital leadership is using the vast reach of technology, especially social media, to improve the lives, well-being and circumstances of others. By blogging we create content to share with others in our PLNs, but also show our students what online interactions should look and sound like.

Sharing your learning with others is powerful. In his book *Innovate Inside the Box: Empowering Learners Through UDL and the Innovator's Mindset* (2019), George Couros believes not only do educators need to be master learners, but they need to reflect on how their new learning will impact other learners. Blogging helps us do this in a seamless way. We share what we learn and make connections to our practice. It is where application meets learning. Every book I read, every lesson I teach, and every experience I have impacts my teaching and blogging gives me a wonderful platform to share all this.

What to Include in a Blog

At the start, I wasn't sure what to write about, so I just reflected on things that were happening in my world. I started off sharing why I was writing a blog. Early posts also focused on things that inspired me, the positive effects of social media, and programs that I amplified in my role.

As I continued blogging, my posts were inspired by many things. Quite a few times, something I heard while listening to a podcast would spark a blog post. Other times, a colleague's story would lead to a post.

One summer, I participated in Blogging Bingo in one of my blogging groups. Participants would select a different topic to blog about each time in an attempt to get BINGO. These posts were collected in a Google Sheet for all the participants to view..

As my second year of blogging began, I started to get even more personal in my blog posts. Embracing the Be REAL mindset, I found these personal reflections benefited me in not only writing but growing as an educator and as a person.

Since then, I have posted a blog almost every week. Some months, I post more and some months less. What hasn't changed is my commitment to sharing my voice through my blog. I don't worry about whether or not anyone reads it, it's for me. But apparently, people have been reading it and that fills my heart with joy.

Expanding Your Blogging Audience

One day while listening to the Teachers on Fire podcast (@TeachersonFire) the host, Tim Cavey (@MisterCavey), announced that any bloggers interested in joining the Teachers on Fire Magazine on Medium should direct message him. I sent him a message and joined the team. Publishing my blog on my own website was great, but when I started posting on Medium, it felt different. Now, someone else was not only reading my posts, but amplifying my voice and my journey.

While posting on the Teachers on Fire Magazine that year I noticed another blogger, Katelynn Giordano (@kngiordano), also posted regularly. So, when I saw that she was being interviewed on the Teach Better Talk podcast, I tuned in to learn more about her. The episode really engaged me. When Katelynn asked the listeners to email her for a chance to guest blog, I sent one that day. Katelynn quickly wrote back. This was an opportunity to share my work with yet another audience.

Later, I attended a School Rubric session during which I noticed School Rubric had contributing writers. After the session I emailed Wallace Ting (@TingWallace), one of the editors, and asked about writing an article. He was receptive and we scheduled a meeting to discuss School Rubric's mission and expectations. I wrote a couple of articles for School Rubric in 2020. They have a fascinating global audience and this allowed me to expand my writing.

I have worked very hard to make my blog a personal history. I enjoy curating content and I have found communities of other educators who share similar goals.

Presenting and Sharing Your Voice

When you blog, you put yourself out there every time you publish. You blog for yourself and if someone else finds value in your words, it's a wonderful feeling. You want to spread your message to an even wider audience.

I decided to challenge myself and applied to speak at local, state and national conferences. Looking back, I am shocked at how bold I was in this decision. With the exception of presenting at a county technology coaches' conference with a colleague and school based professional development sessions, I had never presented before.

I began with another county technology coaches' conference by presenting Empowering Student Voices with Technology Tools. I was nervous about my sessions and each one was packed. It was gratifying to see in the exit tickets that the participants valued my presentation.

One participant said, "Lots of great examples of ways that students can use the tools we already have to demonstrate their learning and their creativity. I saw that one doesn't have to spend hours and hours planning such activities and the projects were things that all students could do."

As I got ready to leave, the conference coordinator, Mike Abrams (@AbramsTank95), came and asked me how things had gone. I declared that it had been a wonderful experience and thanked him for the opportunity. I told him that I almost hadn't put in a proposal. His response shocked me. He said when he saw my proposal, he recognized me from my Twitter feed and knew he wanted me at his conference. I was honored. When you put things out on social media you never know who might see it and how it might affect them.

After this initial success, I started looking for other conferences at which to speak. I brainstormed possible sessions I was interested in presenting. I thought about what I was truly passionate about and what I hadn't seen featured in conferences I had previously attended. Using this list, I wrote abstracts for each session and showed a draft to a few colleagues. It is a good idea to talk to someone in your PLN who has more experience before sending any proposals out. Their feedback was extremely valuable.

I was embracing the idea that you miss 100% of the shots you don't take. I applied to speak at several conferences and eagerly awaited word on whether or not my proposals would be accepted. Much to my delight, I found myself presenting at TECHpalooza in Danville, VA and the Upstate Technology Conference (@upstatetec).

Around this time, closures due to the COVID-19 pandemic had started to happen. Many conferences were being postponed or were made virtual. TECHpalooza suddenly became Teaching with Tech and the Upstate Technology Conference became the Summer of Tech in these virtual adaptations.

Virtual conferences popped up as it became more apparent this situation wasn't changing any time soon. I quickly learned about presenting virtually. It wasn't easy, but I persevered. Then, I was provided another opportunity by School Rubric (@schoolrubric). I was invited to present as part of their Saturday morning professional development. In these sessions, there were two presentations of about 10-12 minutes each followed by questions. These presentations were edited, then presented as webinars.

By the end of that year I had met one of my goals: I presented two sessions at Virginia Society for Technology in Education (VSTE). Although all of my presentations meant a lot to me, presenting at my state conference meant a little bit more. As I looked at the other presenters there, I initially felt like an imposter, but then I realized I had earned the right to be there. What an awesome feeling! My message was resonating and I had challenged myself and reached my goals!

What if? My Book Journey

At one point I participated in a Lead Like a Pirate (LeadLAP) chat featuring questions in which we analyzed the effectiveness of resolutions. Followed by planning how to hold ourselves accountable to these resolutions. This continued with the idea of The Burden of Busy, a blog post by Beth Houf (@BethHouf). One quote resonated with me, "I've realized that when I take time to rest and set limits, I am actually more productive both at home and work."(Houf, 2019) As the chat ended, we were asked to post a call to action.

I paused before I responded. What if I wrote my dreams and not just what I thought were attainable goals? Without overthinking it, I responded: present at conferences and write a book. Jay Billy (@JayBilly2) responded by telling me to just do it.

As the year began, I seriously started thinking about writing a book. One day while walking on the trail near my house, the idea came to me. I wanted to share the story of my transformation, from my start as a floundering teacher to how becoming a connected educator helped me overcome my struggles. I also wanted to share meaningful ways technology could be integrated to amplify and empower student learning. I wanted to share this in the hopes that someone would read my story and get something from it. I have read so many other inspiring educator stories that helped me grow. I wanted to pay it forward.

I started writing and made a lot of progress between January and March. Then the COVID pandemic hit in March 2020. The demands of emergency remote learning took over and drained all of my creative energy. This continued even during the summer months and into the fall. By the time winter break started, I figured I needed to postpone my book journey and add it to my goals for next year.

I had been so preoccupied with setting goals for the next year, I almost forgot I still had a few days left in the current year to challenge myself. Rather than focusing on the last couple of days of this year, I was attempting to jump forward into the new year without giving myself any last chances to reach my goals!

On Saturday, December 26, 2020, a thought struck me as I watched a Teachers On Fire Round Table discussion. Tim Cavey (@MisterCavey) was interviewing authors about their writing process and asked if they had any advice for aspiring writers. I was absorbed in this discussion. I knew Rachelle Dene Poth (@Rdene915) already from her books and her blog, but the other authors, Jillian DuBois (@JillDuBois22) and David Frangiosa (@DavidFrangiosa) were new to me. Listening to the authors' processes was illuminating and led me to several realizations.

During the discussion, I posted a question in the chat asking if the authors had finished their book draft completely before sending it to a publisher. I was surprised to hear that it depended on the publisher. Some publishers wanted more of a proposal or pitch, while others wanted a more than 50% completed draft. I thought I probably had enough to send out. When Rachelle said she thought I had a book in me, I was touched. I appreciated how Rachelle amplified other educators in her blog and was honored she posted four of my blogs as guest posts.

Blogging helped those authors find their audience and would do the same for me. Each author explained how blogging was an important part of their writing journey. When I started blogging, I wasn't sure anyone would read my blog or care about what I had to say. John Meehan (@MeehanEDU) shared an inspirational thought in a pd4uandme bloggers message group. Tweeting leads to blogging. Blogging leads to presenting. Presenting leads to book chapters, and book chapters lead to things like this [his first book being released. As I reflected on John's words, I knew I was ready for the final step. I could do this. I had book chapters ready and I could send in my proposal now.

During the Round Table, I wrote down the names of the publishers who had published these authors' works. I then checked to see if I was ready to send a proposal to any of them. Jillian DuBois said she sent her children's book to several publishers that didn't work out.

Then, she took a chance and sent it to one more publisher who loved her work. So, as Tara Martin (@TaraMartinEDU) says, I cannonballed in and sent my proposal to three publishers and was exhilarated to hear back from all three.

Writing a book was a dream for me. Sending it out to publishers was the ultimate challenge for me that year. This ignited my passion for writing like nothing else. During winter break, I was inspired to write every day. This continued into the next year with my commitment to write at least 30 minutes per day.

Writing daily took the overwhelmed feeling away from me. It became part of my self care and I worked to finish my manuscript. It redefined my journey and led me to focus on what I loved so much about education. I took the professional step of getting a domain name, www.tannenbaumtech.com, and completely redesigned my website. These steps made me feel empowered.

Don't be afraid to take that leap. We all have a story to tell. Not only will it empower you, but imagine the impact on others who hear your story. You never know how one action can affect another person, but as educators isn't that one of our greatest gifts?

Post a Techy Note

Share how you can offer your voice and share your story using #transform.

Chapter 8
Reach Beyond Your Expectations

My #oneword2020 was CHALLENGE. I wanted to challenge myself to take risks, try new things. I needed to eat healthy and mindfully and exercise regularly. I wanted to read, learn and reflect regularly. I wanted to take risks by speaking at conferences and writing a book.

These challenges began a year-long journey of self improvement. They dared me to reach beyond what I had previously expected of myself and push out of my comfort zone. This was not easy for me, but I lived by this word and incorporated it in both my professional and personal life.

Professional CHALLENGE

I presented at ten virtual conferences during the year. I worked on a draft of this book and sent it to a couple of publishers. I blogged and even contributed to other blogs and publications. In fact, I was asked and later selected to be a contributing author in an upcoming book. I became a Teach Better Ambassador and a Pear Deck Regional Coach. I worked with my staff navigating a COVID-19 world and saw tremendous growth, dedication and risk-taking among my colleagues. I participated in two Dave Burgess Consulting book clubs to build my culturally proficient mindset. In the process I learned a lot about myself and the world around me. I definitely challenged myself professionally that year and I was proud of the strides I had made.

Personal CHALLENGE

I wanted to be healthier and more active. This was easier said than done. I ended the year heavier than I started it, but along the way I trained and ran a 5 kilometer race. Later in the year, I contracted COVID and all of my progress reversed. Although I was sick for only two weeks with a relatively mild case, it took me much longer to feel normal again. I also navigated many life changes. My son graduated from high school, applied to college and finished his freshman semester at West Virginia University. My daughter finished middle school and started high school. My husband and I moved his parents down from New York to be closer to us. We helped my stepdaughter navigate the struggles of virtual learning. It was definitely a challenging year.

Why CHALLENGE?

You might wonder why CHALLENGE was so important to me that year. The previous year, I attended ISTE19 in Philadelphia. As weird as it may sound, that was the first time I had traveled on my own in close to 20 years. I was so excited about this opportunity, but nervous as well.

I can be pretty shy. So, on the first Sunday of the conference getting ready to go get lunch, I didn't know where to go. However, I stepped out of my shell and asked some other participants where they were going and then asked to join them. As a result, I met some wonderful educators from South Carolina who are now part of my PLN. After that initial victory, I gained confidence. I gain insight from each new conversation I participated in and connected with a lot of people. None of that would have happened if I had never had that first conversation.

Attending ISTE was full of me trying new things and challenging myself. I went to social events each night. From the @EduPodnet meetups to #FlipgridLive to EdTech Karaoke, each experience was unique and unfamiliar, but I appreciated all of them.

Ripple Effect

In Episode 186 of Teach Better Talk (2020), Jeff Gargas and Rae Hughart interviewed Jen Manly, a computer science teacher in Maryland. She said learning should be joyful and talked about ways she empowered students in her classroom. What really struck me was her advice, "If you don't apply, the answer is always no."

I really have tried to model challenging myself for my family, my students and my colleagues. I hoped by modeling this mindset it would rub off on others around me. I watched many people around me take on challenges throughout the year.

This became increasingly clear to me during a conversation with my eighteen year old son that summer. We were discussing a trip to visit some of our estranged relatives. I was nervous about this proposed trip, fearing the impact these toxic relatives could have on him. He said that he knew this trip was a risk, but I had raised him to challenge himself and grow from it. He had noticed me doing the same and that empowered him to accept challenges. He explained that was why he had chosen to participate in a sports management program for the National Student Leadership Conference at Fordham one summer and why he had chosen to attend West Virginia University despite all the uncertainties in the fall. As I listened to him talk, a huge sense of pride overwhelmed me.

Thinking of Jen Manly's quote made me reflect on how mature my son sounded during this conversation. I also thought about some of the recent challenges in my own personal and professional life, especially as I got ready to push send on a very important application to the Google Virtual Innovator Academy.

Turning a "Fail" Around During CHALLENGE

Tim Cavey, from the Teachers on Fire Podcast, invited me to one of his Instagram Live sessions at 3:00 pm. I was amped up and was by my computer ready to go. That was my first misstep. I didn't know that Instagram Live had to be accessed from a mobile device. I then tried my phone. Unfortunately, Instagram chose that afternoon to not work on my phone. By now it is 3:10 or 3:15 and I am getting frustrated.

Here I am a technology coach and am unable to join an Instagram Live! I was feeling pretty pathetic. In desperation I ran into my 14 year old daughter's room and said, "I need your phone for 10 to 15 minutes!" She looked at me like I was crazy, but still handed me her phone. I quickly downloaded Instagram, logged in and was finally able to participate in my first Instagram Live. Tim Cavey never gave up on me. He continued to talk and interact with everyone who was on, giving me lots of tips as I went along. We discussed what I was currently learning. (Apparently, I need to learn more about Instagram, right?) I explained I was learning a lot about how to support my teachers in distance learning and my hope to share some asynchronous tools with my colleagues this week.

The next morning, I instructed seven of my colleagues on Pear Deck. Some were able to get started right away, but not everyone. I am sure a few of my colleagues felt like they were falling flat on their face. I understood that feeling after my own experience the previous day. I took a step back and worked with my colleagues to help them learn more about this technology. With time and a little extra help, they would be successful.

Learning From Setbacks on Your Journey

Turning failure around is never easy. I believe it helps all of us not only grow, but develop empathy for others. I hoped sharing my misstep built up my colleagues. Who knows, maybe someone will read this and build up the courage to try something new and turn around a failure of their own.

Applying to be a Google Certified Innovator was one of my big goals. I had been all set to apply for the Sunnyvale cohort when I learned there would be just one virtual academy that year. I had been working hard to get my application ready, which in and of itself, required many tasks and challenges. One of the first was asking some of my colleagues to be interviewed for my project. Six took time out of their summer vacations to meet virtually with me and share challenges they faced in their classrooms. Listening to their challenges was enlightening and gave me much to think about as I worked on narrowing down my topic from five main categories.

I decided to focus on empowering student agency using technology, since this was an area about which I was already passionate. I intended to use what I learned from these informative conversations to plan for the upcoming school year. With a focus identified, I filled out the application using one teacher's interview as my main focal point.

As I worked, I drafted my responses in a Google document, then reached out to some Google Innovators for feedback. I was appreciative of Stephanie Howell (@mrshowell24) and Theresa Hoover (@MusicalTheresa) for taking the time to contact me. I used their insights to make the necessary changes to my document. I also started on my 90 second video to complete my application. I will be perfectly honest, I hate videoing myself, but I did it anyway.

I started by narrating the challenge I was addressing while using graphics to support my message. Then, I added graphics to overlay my 30 second introduction video. Finally, I recorded my 30 second introduction video segment. This was definitely the hardest part for me to complete, but I did it!

Getting all of your thoughts into a 90 second video is not easy, but after many takes I was finally happy with the result. After I attached it to my application it was time to submit the entire application. I thought to myself, "What's the worst that can happen? They could say no, but what if they say yes?"

What if they say yes? That had been my mindset throughout the summer and that year in general. When Teach Better Ambassador applications opened, I applied. I was thrilled when I became one of the first 25 ambassadors. Earlier that summer, I applied for the ISTE Digital Storytelling Summit, Virtual VSTE and Teaching with Tech Online Summit. I was honored to be selected and all of my sessions went great.

My Google Virtual Innovator Academy (VIA20) Google Innovator Project was not chosen. However, I was fine with this because I learned so much from the process. The experience would allow me to be better prepared the next time applications open.

Next Step: TRANSFORMATION

The next year, I wanted to take all the strides I had made through CHALLENGE to the next level. I wanted to push myself further to be the best me I could be. I chose TRANSFORMATION as my word for this reason.

Before deciding on this word, I attended Lindsay Titus' Word Party, (@ltitus828). The virtual event was intended to help people discover the one word for this year that inspires them (#oneword2021). We reflected on the previous year, then were asked to imagine our current year using feelings, thoughts and achievements. How did I want to feel and think and what did I want to achieve in this year?

Feelings

I wanted to feel healthy and be energetic. I wanted to feel proud of the choices I made, and feel renewed and fresh. I wanted to wake up each morning ready to approach my day and feel grateful for all the blessings in my life.

I also wanted to feel accomplished. I wanted to not only feel successful and appreciated in my work, but more connected to the educational community and it's work. Like the Teach Better mindset, I wanted to feel like I was better every day than I was the day before.

Thoughts

I wanted to focus on improved health with mindful eating and an active lifestyle. I wanted to include gratitude as a daily component of my life and think of the glass as half full. I wanted to have a growth mindset, knowing there would be bumps along the way, but still reach my goals.

I also wanted to set aside time each day to finish my book and find just the right publisher. I wanted to set aside more time to connect with others. I wanted to find ways to listen and learn more and use what I discovered to help me become a better educator.

Achievements

I wanted to get back to a healthy weight. I wanted to run another half marathon and beat my personal record. I wanted to travel with my husband, when it was safe to do so again. I wanted to see at least one Broadway show with my daughter. I wanted to enjoy family events and treasure those I loved.

I also wanted to continue to speak at conferences. I wanted to take my blog up a notch, get a domain name and create a mailing list. However, the biggest thing I wanted to achieve was to finish my book and get it published.

A Mindset and a Mantra

I viewed my #oneword2021 as a mindset and a mantra. I would work each day to fully transform the challenges I faced in the previous year.

To live the mantra every day I would:
- Be active by getting 10,000 steps a day
- Learn something new by reading every day
- Be healthy by eating mindfully
- Reflect and grow by writing every day in some manner
- Blog regularly and update my blog weekly

- Live the TRANSFORM mindset by pushing past my comfort zone to reach my goals

I set up a new journal so I could monitor these goals daily. Journaling became part of my regular schedule. Each day I updated my progress on these goals while also taking some time to record gratitude notes and a daily reflection.

Each morning began with reading from an educational book for 10-15 minutes to learn something. This was followed by 30 minutes of writing, either journaling or writing my book. Next, my dog and I took a walk, followed by eating a healthy breakfast. All of this happened each day before 7:30 am. I began my days with a sense of accomplishment which changed the entire trajectory of my day.

Many of us begin each day hearing doubts in our heads and our goal is to tread water and survive. Imagine what could happen if we began each day with accomplishment? What if we took those successes and pushed just a little bit further and considered the What If. What if I try something new, what if I apply for something that seems slightly out of reach, what if I take a risk? Two things can happen, it might work out or it might not. You won't know until you try, so why not go and see? You'll be amazed at the transformations you might see.

Post a Techy Note

Share what happens when you take a risk using #transform.

Chapter 9

Maximize Learning Anywhere, Anytime

After enduring the unprecedented school years of 2019-2020 and 2020-2021, one thing should be clear, not only are educators resilient and creative, but capable of growth beyond anyone's expectations. This was not inspired by the need to raise test scores or a district mandate, but by the love educators hold for their students. Educators want the best for their students and have dedicated hours beyond hours to give their students what they need.

New Approaches to Professional Learning

We have demonstrated that student learning can happen anywhere and at any time. In many ways this starts with professional development. Like classroom instruction, professional development transformed during these two years. No longer were educators confined to a location to learn, technology afforded them the ability to learn anything, anywhere. As a technology coach, it was exciting to see the creative approaches to professional development that emerged and the ripple effect that occurred afterwards.

Professional Development Revealed Unsung Heroes

The idea for summer learning opportunities started as a response to our end of the year distance learning survey for teachers. As the assistant principal and I reviewed data from the surveys, a few primary needs stood out. Teachers wanted to learn how to make synchronous learning more engaging and effective, more about tools they were already familiar with, more about Pear Deck, and ways to build relationships in virtual classrooms.

In response, the summer learning opportunities schedule was born. It provided staff with differentiated ways to learn about technology tools they were familiar with while also providing opportunities to learn about technology to promote community and relationship building.

I was honored to host sixteen summer learning opportunities in just eight days. If one word could describe how I felt about this week it would be WOW! I worked with some of the most dedicated educators I have ever met. Each of my sessions had 15-25 participants. Many of my colleagues attended multiple sessions and one dedicated individual even attended them all! Contracted work days didn't begin until the Friday after the summer sessions, but these teachers were ready to add to their virtual learning toolbox on their own time.

The first week started with introductory sessions. One session taught the basics of Google Classroom. Since I am passionate about our youngest learners using Google Classroom, I was excited to see so many primary teachers, instructional assistants and special education teachers join. In another session we reviewed the basics of our synchronous learning system, Blackboard Collaborate Ultra. Once again, I was thrilled to see so many of my colleagues eager to learn about this tool to connect with their students.

As the week continued, the number of staff members attending continued to grow. We explored Pear Deck and Google Slides. I watched with joy as my colleagues discovered all of the superpowers embedded in these programs. We discussed ways to increase student to student engagement through things like Flipgrid, interactive slides and Padlet. It was exciting to see so many people not only ready to learn, but dedicated to being the best they could be. This pushed me to be my best!

Sessions I had created in the spring were a great starting point, but if I wanted to help my colleagues increase their student to student interactions, I needed to model these interactions with them. I used breakout rooms and partnered them up with collaborative Slide Decks, Padlets and more. I used Flipgrid to build synchronous connections. They became Pear Deck proficient and adept at using Slides in new ways.

As week one concluded, the assistant principal and I got started scheduling the upcoming week. Two teachers had volunteered to host some of these sessions. We encouraged teachers to attend Pear Fair, a free professional development event hosted by Pear Deck. We also decided to add sessions on Padlet, Wixie and HyperDocs. I pushed myself to see how I could model the interactivity teachers had asked about in their end of the year surveys.

I was proud to be part of my school's learning community and of the impact of my position. Every day, I helped others leverage technology to amplify student learning. In a virtual learning environment, it was no longer just about learning the technology, but what opportunities the technology provided to connect and engage our students.

Some of my most powerful insights occurred as I reviewed the attendance data. About 25% of the participants were instructional assistants. They were eager to learn. Here was a group of educators who normally don't get to participate in professional development, but these training sessions empowered them to learn. This was transformational in the fall. It created a situation where our instructional assistants were partners in our classrooms, both virtually and face to face.

Powerful Learning from Anywhere

One of my goals during the previous year was to challenge myself to speak more at conferences. I wanted to share my ideas and knowledge with a greater audience, in addition to continuing my educational journey and learning from others. As social distancing became the norm, traveling and attending conferences became a nonstarter.

As I mentioned before, this did not stop educators. Around the world educators rose to the challenge and created innovative platforms for virtual conferences. Although this virtual experience could not replicate the in person feeling that comes from attending conferences and EdCamps, they provided educators with many learning opportunities.

Having four children, one of them in college, virtual conferences gave me an opportunity to present in places that would have been cost prohibitive otherwise. I presented at ten different conferences varying in location from Oregon to Tennessee to South Carolina to my home state of Virginia. Not only did this help me become a better speaker, the knowledge I gained while attending these conferences was immeasurable.

Conferences were not the only way educators rose to the challenge during these times. Educators began hosting more live streams and sharing content to a variety of social media platforms through programs like Streamyard.

The Teach Better Team hosted two 12 hour events of live, free professional development to platforms such as Facebook, Twitter, Twitch and YouTube. Events like these were phenomenal. The Teach Better Team compiled an extensive program, bringing educators together to share their knowledge and interact with the audience. As a Teach Better Ambassador, I was proud to be linked to an organization that created such wonderful events.

The ThriveinEDU community also hosted regularly scheduled events to gather educators together. From biweekly events like Thrive O'Clock to Ugly Sweater parties, Rachelle Dene Poth and Melody McAllister created a feeling of community in times when people felt alone.

Tim Cavey, of the Teachers on Fire podcast and community, also began hosting weekly Roundtable events where he invited a panel of educators each Saturday morning to discuss a variety of topics. These were quick and informative bursts of inspiration needed by educators during these trying times.

The Lead Like a Pirate (LeadLAP) community also capitalized on this innovation. At this point in the year, many educators were inspired to become allies to the Black Lives Matter movement. Shelley Burgess and Beth Houf, creators of LeadLAP, along with Tracy Browder and Dawn Harris took a traditional Saturday morning Twitter chat and transformed it using weekly video introductions. They created a community and even did their Twitter chats in conjunction with a live Zoom meeting.

Dave Burgess Consulting held book clubs through Zoom for culturally relevant books like *White Fragility* (DiAngelo, 2018) and *Culturally Responsive Teaching and the Brain: Promoting Authentic Engagement and Rigor Among Culturally and Linguistically Diverse Students* (Hammond, 2014) that connected educators across the country in dialogue led by the amazing Marisol Rerucha. During these weekly discussion groups participants, like myself, engaged in meaningful yet difficult discussions that enabled all of us to learn more about ourselves and others.

These were the tip of the iceberg when it came to the transformation of professional development in 2020, but the lessons learned through this experience were clear. Teachers did not need to travel to learn. Virtual options for conferences in the future are a great way to provide teachers who either can't afford the cost or leave time required by many larger educational conferences. You don't need to attend a conference to learn.

New Approaches in the Classrooms

Professional development was not the only place advances happened during the 2019-2020 and 2020-2021 school years. Many classrooms around the nation were transformed as well.

Pear Decking

One particular morning, I received several emails that lit me up inside. When I received these emails, I knew that not only had I inspired their senders, but I needed to publish in my blog the positive influence these colleagues were having on me.

The first email was from one of my teachers. This teacher proclaimed herself technologically adjacent and struggled using technology. I was so excited when I saw her join my Pear Deck learning opportunity the week prior. I knew she was taking a risk and I was so glad she had taken time to join me. Imagine my delight when I read her email. She had Pear Decked that morning!

Many times after a training, new skills learned can sit stagnant. But less than 24 hours later, this teacher had put them into action and shared her victory with me. I was supposed to go to her class the following day to model Pear Deck in her classroom. It was great that her students had already Pear Decked!

The second email took me by surprise. It was from one of our art teachers who had not attended any of my Pear Deck trainings yet. She had visited another teacher's class in which I had previously modeled Pear Deck. Once again, less than 24 hours after this session, the art teacher created her own Pear Deck lesson and shared it with her students.

I emailed the teacher to let her know she had inspired our art teacher and to ask her how it went. SIt had gone well and she wondered if she could stop by during my office hours to ask a few follow up questions. I couldn't wait to see where she led her class next. I also replied to the art teacher's email. I wanted her to know how excited I was that she would be joining me the following Tuesday for our next Pear Deck training. I could only imagine the possibilities of Pear Decking in an art class. The art teacher explained that she had each student draw a picture with a message about art class. It touched my heart when I saw what they drew on their slides.

The third email I received was from one of our special education teachers. She wrote that she was planning on Pear Decking a lesson about social skills with her students. She had also attended a previous Pear Deck session. She was so excited to engage her students in some of the perspective taking slides.

The Power of Video

One grade level team in my school became video masters. Rather than relying on synchronous lessons, they curated a library of instructional videos to help their students learn anywhere, anytime.

One teacher led this effort with pre-recorded math videos. No matter what they were learning about, her videos engaged the students. She gave them instructions on when to pause the video to try to work the problem, then resume the video. She used a combination of live video, powerpoint slides and video clips to engage her students virtually. Even as an adult, I found myself raptly watching these videos. Every activity had a follow up activity for the students to work on as a check in afterwards.

This entire team was new to video prior to the extended closure, but they learned to embrace it. All of this hard work gave them the opportunity to flip instruction for their young students.

Staying Informed with Google Forms

Another grade level team also embraced ways to connect with their students asynchronously. Their students completed end of the week reflections each Friday using Google Forms.

Students recorded not only how much effort they were putting into their daily assignments, but also how focused and productive they were during distance learning. The reflection was concluded by setting a goal for the following week.

Using this information, teachers monitored their students' engagement from the previous week as well as their current week's goals. Students built their metacognitive skills as they self-evaluated during distance learning. The teachers acknowledged that distance learning requires a lot of perseverance and time management and used these reflections as a way to connect to their learners and empower them.

Using Google Sites to House a Virtual Library

Our fabulous librarian, Nicole Oberdick (@MrsOberdick), missed her students during remote teaching. Unlike classroom teachers, specialists initially did not have the opportunity to connect synchronously with students. Mrs. Oberdick accomplished this by creating a Google site to house her virtual library. She not only shared library resources, but she also had library lessons for students and reading Choice Boards. She read aloud for the students' enjoyment and had a webpage for parent resources. She created a virtual space students and staff could visit, much like her physical library, to find resources and learn more about books.

Teachers are not only dedicated but resilient. They accept challenges and see opportunities to grow and learn. When I started teaching in the late 1990s, teachers taught behind closed doors and the job was isolating. Now we live in a connected world that affords us so many ways to learn, connect, share, and create anywhere at any time.

Are you taking advantage of all of these opportunities or holding back? How can you transform your journey? Will you...

- **T**urn away from a closed door approach?
- **R**evisit how you use technology in your class?
- **A**mplify learning with technology tools?
- **N**urture and empower student agency?
- **S**eek connections outside of your school?
- **F**ind your PLN?
- **O**ffer your voice and share your story?
- **R**each beyond your expectations?
- **M**aximize learning anywhere, anytime?

Will you find your own unique path of transformation instead?

Post a Techy Note

I hope the stories shared in this book inspire you to go for it. I'd love to hear from you. Tag me @TannenbaumTech and use #transform on Twitter. After all, we are all better together.

Works Cited

Bell, K. (2018). Shake Up Learning: Practice Ideas to Move from Static to Dynamic. Dave Burgess Consulting, Inc.

Casa-Todd, J. (2017). Social LEADia. Dave Burgess Consulting Inc, 2017.

CAST. (2018). Universal Design for Learning Guidelines version 2.2. The UDL Guidelines. https://udlguidelines.cast.org/

Couros, G., & Novak, K. (2019). Innovate Inside the Box-Empowering Learning Through UDL and the Innovator's Mindset. IMPress.

Creative Educator. (2014). Students as eBook Authors. Literacy. Retrieved May 2, 2021, from https://creativeeducator.tech4learning.com/2014/articles/Authentic-Authors-with-ePubs

Czyz, R. (2017). The Four O'Clock Faculty: A Rogue Guide to Revolutionizing Professional Development. Dave Burgess Consulting Inc.

Davis, V. (2018, Nov 7). How do I help my students use iPads? Teaching students to troubleshoot and use iPads effectively (388).The Ten Minute Teacher Podcast. CoolCatTeacher. https://www.coolcatteacher.com/e388

Gale- A Cengage Company. (n.d.). Gale in Content: Elementary. Gale in Content: Elementary. https://go.gale.com/ps/start.do? p=ITKE&u=fairfaxcps&sid=geolinks

Gargas, J. and Hughart, R. (2020, July 1). Learning Should be Joyful. (186). In Teach Better Talk. https://www.teachbetter.com/podcast/ jenmanly/attachment/teach-better-talk-episode-186

Hammond, Z. L. (2015). Culturally Responsive Teaching and the Brain. Corwin.

Hare, R. (2020). Practical Creativity: How to Recognize and Cultivate it in Your School [Keynote for Adobe Creative Educator Day]. McLean, VA.

Harvard Graduate School of Education. (2016). Project Zero's Thinking Routine Toolbox. Project Zero. http://www.pz.harvard.edu/ thinking-routines

Highfill, L., Hilton, K., & Landis, S. (2016). The Hyperdocs Handbook: Digital Lesson Design Using Google Apps. Elevate Books
        EDU.

Houf, B. (2019). The Burden of Busy. Lead Like a Pirate. Retrieved 12 28, 2019, from https://leadlikeapirate.net/the-burden-of-busy/

Kelley, D. (2019, February 18). David Kelley on the 8 Design Abilities of Creative Problem Solvers. Visual Media Alliance- Education. Retrieved October 3, 2020, from https://education.vma.bz/general/ david-kelley-on-the-8-design-abilities-of-creative-problem-solvers

Mahan, B. (2018, May 29). *The ADHD Essentials Podcast with Brendan Mahan, M.Ed., M.S.* ADHD Essentials. https://www.adhdessentials.com/podcasts/

Martin, T. (2018). BE REAL: Educate from the Heart. Dave Burgess Consulting Inc.

Merriam-Webster. (n.d.). Create. In Merriam-Webster.com dictionary. Retrieved May 13, 2021, from https://www.merriam-webster.com/dictionary/create

Ritchart, R. (2021). Graphics Related to the 8 Cultural Forces. Ron Ritchart. https://www.ronritchhart.com/info-graphics

Spencer, J. (2020). Empowered at a Distance. Blend Education.

Tech4Learning. (2021). Creating Comics in the Elementary School Classroom. Wixie. https://static.wixie.com/edu/comics-elementary

Vincent, T. (2019). Shapegrams. Shapegrams .https://shapegrams.com/

About the Author

Debbie Tannenbaum is a School Based Technology Specialist in an elementary school in Fairfax County, Virginia. An educator with over twenty years of experience, Debbie Tannenbaum supports both staff and students to integrate technology tools into instruction through co-teaching sessions and weekly technology classes. Debbie emphasizes working collaboratively with other educators to use technology tools that amplify student learning and empower student voice in all of her interactions with both students and fellow educators.

Outside of school, Debbie blogs and shares her experiences as a technology coach through her thoughts and reflections regularly on her website: https://www.tannenbaumtech.com. In her blogs, she shares encouragement, inspiration and a variety of technology resources to empower educators to make meaningful changes in their teaching practice. Readers will note her honesty and vulnerability in sharing her journey.

In addition, Debbie actively shares on social media and loves connecting with other educators. She adds to her connections regularly by speaking at conferences across the country and beyond including ISTE, MASSCUE, VSTE, and CUE. In her presentations, she focuses on the opportunities technology tools provide and ways they can transform learning for both students and educators..

Debbie loves learning and truly embodies the mindset of a lifelong learner. She shares this zeal with her husband, Joe, and her four children, Jacob, Mollie, Josh and Ali, and her dog, Brisket. Her family, especially her husband, has always championed her and encouraged her to go after her dreams. They are her heroes behind the scenes and she is dedicated to them always.

Connect with Debbie on Twitter and Instagram: @TannenbaumTech.

TRANSFORM AND AMPLIFY LEARNING WITH TANNENBAUMTECH

KEYNOTE SESSION: TRANSFORM-Techy Notes to Make Learning Sticky

Based on *TRANSFORM: Techy Notes to Make Learning Sticky*, this keynote focuses on:

1. Discovering " TRANSFORM" tech tools that offer your students new and innovative ways to learn

2. Implementing these tech tools to focus on creation and to promote student agency

3. Empowering yourself using technology tools to make your professional learning sticky.

BREAKOUT SESSIONS

1. **Amplifying Thinking Routines with Technology Tools**
    *   Learn about the impact of Project Zero's Thinking Routines
    *   Discover when and how using technology tools can amplify the use of these routines.

    *

2. **Creating with Littles**

- Discover easy ways to promote student agency.

- Learn ways digital tools can provide our students amazing opportunities to create.

3. **Empowering Student Voice with Technology Tools**

- Discover easy ways to use technology tools to give your students opportunities to share their voices in interactive ways.

TECHNOLOGY COACHING

Using technology to transform learning can seem daunting, but it doesn't have to be. It just requires intentional planning to make sure the technology truly transforms instruction. Set up a free consultation and see how working with Debbie and her TRANSFORM framework can amplify student learning for your class, school or district.

More from Road to Awesome

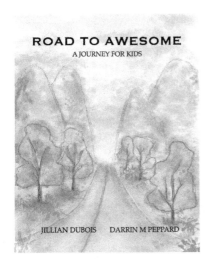

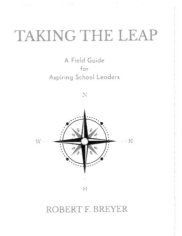

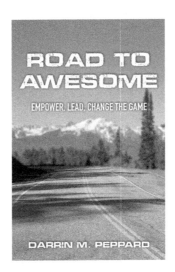

(Via Codebreaker)

ROAD TO
AWESOME

Made in the USA
Middletown, DE
09 October 2023

40321955R00109